FROM THE FLAMES

FROM THE FLAMES

MIRACLES AND WONDERS OF SURVIVAL

William Hauben

Writers Club Press
San Jose New York Lincoln Shanghai

From the Flames
Miracles and Wonders of Survival

Writers Club Press
an imprint of iUniverse.com, Inc.

For information address:
iUniverse.com, Inc.
5220 S 16th, Ste. 200
Lincoln, NE 68512
www.iuniverse.com

ISBN: 0-595-15865-X

Printed in the United States of America

I. Hauben, William. 2. Holocaust survivors-
Biography. 3. Jews-Poland-Krakow-Biography.
4. Holocaust, Jewish (1939-1945)-Poland-Krakow-Personal narratives. 5. Holocaust, Jewish (1939-1945)-Austria- Personal narratives. 6. Ebensee (Concentration camp)
I. Title.

Note to the reader: As a living witness, I have tried to the best of my ability to recapture the events surrounding my early life and experiences during the war years. Resources have been used to round out my memory of events, some of which detail eyewitness accounts of others that are part of the history of the Holocaust.

To my beloved parents, Solomon & Gertrude Hauben, and my only brother, Abraham (Romek) Hauben, Z"L of blessed memory. And to my beloved wife, Brina (Bracha), Z"L of blessed memory.

And, in commemoration of Kristallnacht, November 9-10, 1938, I dedicate this book to the blessed memory of our lost Jewish culture.

How Can I Repay the Lord for All His Gifts to Me?

I Will Raise the Cup of Deliverance,
And Invoke the Lord by Name.

I Will Pay My Vows to the Lord in the Presence of All His People.

Grievous in the Sight of the Lord Is the Death of His Faithful.

I Am Your Servant, Born of Your Maidservant;
You Have Released Me from Bondage.

To You Will I Bring an Offering, and Invoke the Lord by Name.

My Vows to the Lord Will I Pay in the Presence of All His People,

In the Courts of the House of the Lord
In the Midst of Jerusalem, Halleluyah.

Psalm 116: 12-19

Contents

Acknowledgments

I feel a great sense of genuine pleasure in thanking my associate, Marian Bruin, for her commitment and sincere loyalty. She has given of her time and energy in helping to make my dream possible, for a cause she truly believed in.

A special thanks to Sally Axelrod, a woman of valor, for all the magnificent work and guidance she provided.

A special salute to my brother-in-law, Morris Stein, for formulating my manuscript and inspiring me.

To Kathy Fountain and Glenn Selig of Channel 13 WTVT television, Tampa, Florida, for giving me the idea to write the story of my life, and of my accomplishments. My sincere thanks to you.

To Todd and Lee Mezrah and my former Bar and Bat Mitzvah students (1969-1990) for their generous support.

To Professor Carolyn Johnston for her sincere and heartfelt cooperation. And to Bonnie Ganderson and Cheryl Gleghorn, who provided much needed editorial assistance and support.

I gratefully acknowledge Rabbi Marc Sack, Cantor Moshe Friedler, Dr. Bernard Germain, Dr. Morris Hanan, Dr. Martin Port, Dr. Joachim Scharf, James E. Tokley, Sr., Barry A. Cohen, Esq., Warren Harris, Esq., Dr. Bernard Hochberg, Dr. Stephen Kreitzer, Dr. John West, Dr. Bernard Stein, Dr. Byron Verkauf, Dr. Felix LoCicero, Arline Verkauf, and Louis Morris, honorary president of Rodeph Sholom Congregation, Tampa, Florida.

I hereby acknowledge Greetings from the Florida Holocaust Museum and Educational Center, St. Petersburg, Florida, from the following dedicated individuals: Walter Loebenberg, founder; John Loftus, president, Larry Wasser, executive director, Stephen Goldman, museum director, and from the Tampa Rabbinical Association president Rabbi Joel Wasser, and the Pinellas County Board of Rabbis, Rabbi Gabriel Ben Or, president.

I would like to express my heartfelt gratitude to the former rabbis and leadership of Rodeph Sholom Congregation for their cooperation throughout the years: past presidents Leo Levinson Z"L, Sol Walker Z"L, Eugene Eisen Z"L, Paul Buchman Z"L, Eugene Linsky, David Shear, Esq., Sam Bobo, Sam Verkauf, Howard Sinsely, Louis Morris, Michael Levine, Bernice Wolf, Martin Solomon, Rabbi Stanley Kazan, Rabbi Sandford Hahn, Rabbi Martin Sandberg, Rabbi Theodore Brod, Rabbi Kenneth Berger Z"L (of blessed memory), and Rabbi Hillel Millgram.

The Cantors Assembly of the Jewish Theological Seminary of America extends warmest personal Greetings and sincere appreciation to all those associated with this project for their unique contributions to the lifeblood of American and world Jewry. I wish to thank Abraham B. Shapiro, Hazzan and Executive Administrator of the Cantors Assembly for his good wishes on my behalf.

A Note From the Editor

When I was introduced to William Hauben in 1997, I knew only that he was a retired cantor and a Holocaust survivor. He seemed a bit eccentric, and I wondered about the stories he had to tell. I agreed to meet with him weekly to help shape his memoirs into readable form.

Every Sunday he would bring a bag containing little packages of candy and specialty foods, each neatly wrapped in plastic and stapled at the ends. He would also bring one or two special items from his vast collection and proceed to tell me the history and significance of each piece. He recorded everything with photographs, legal documents, newspaper articles, etc. His stories inevitably brought me to tears.

For this baby boomer with Jewish roots, William represented an untapped encyclopedia of Hebraic knowledge: how, as a survivor of four Nazi slave labor camps, he was fluent in seven languages, had served as a cantor for over 30 years, and had extensive knowledge of Jewish liturgical and theater music. He was a musician and an electrician, a translator and an archivist. I was quite simply in awe of him.

These memoirs document some of the most unbelievable travesties in human existence. Upon his liberation from Ebensee Concentration Camp, William knew that he had survived for a single purpose: that his mission in life was to salvage and preserve Jewish historical items. In 1998, The William Hauben Heritage Foundation, Inc., a nonprofit 501(c)(3) organization was incorporated in the State of Florida. The purpose of the Foundation is to educate people around the world about the Holocaust and the history and culture of the Jewish people. A collection of rare books, coins, photographs, documents, and other items from seven European countries have been catalogued and are available for exhibit.

I often have asked myself how I would have weathered such experiences as those the author describes. I believe I would have lacked the kind of faith and determination that William had to survive. It has been a unique privilege to work with him.

Marian Bruin
The William Hauben Heritage
Foundation, Inc.
May 2000

Preface

And the Lord said to Abram, "Go forth from your native land and from your father's house to the land that I will show you.

> "I will make of you a great nation,
> And I will bless you;
> I will make your name great,
> And you shall be a blessing.
> I will bless those who bless you
> And curse him that curses you;
> And all the families of the earth
> Shall bless themselves by you."
>
> Genesis 12:1-3

And so a nation was born. Out of the ashes of despair and destruction of a demonic despot, the State of Israel emerged victorious, a spiritual homeland for the Jewish people, a beacon of light for the trampled and oppressed, a vision of eternal hope for those who survived. Surely one of G-d's miracles.

My own personal story begins as a young boy in Cracow, Poland, born of two loving parents who wanted nothing but the best for their two young sons, only to see it all destroyed in front of their very own eyes.

As is the case with survivors whose stories have come before me, "bearing witness" is an obligation that most of us who have survived the Holocaust want to share, to tell the world what we experienced in the hope that the horror we endured will never be repeated. With G-d's divine intervention we have kept the memory alive, lest we forget, not only the terror of the war years, but the human goodness of Righteous Persons who risked their own lives to save ours.

The question persists: How could it have happened? How was it possible for a modern state to carry out the systematic murder of a whole people for no reason other than that they were Jews? How was it possible for a whole people to allow itself to be destroyed? How was it possible for the world to stand by without halting this destruction? [1]

Ethnic violence and hostility between Christians and Jews is ancient, but the Holocaust stands out as the only systematic effort by a modern government to destroy an entire people. The history books tell us that Hitler believed all other races were inferior, that the Germans were pure-blooded Aryans, a master race destined to rule the world. The bulk of European Jewry were destroyed solely because of the fanatic Nazi belief that Jews were the carriers of genetic inheritance that mortally threatened German and Christian values. Hitler wanted the whole world, starting with Europe, *judenrein,* a place without Jews. With this pathological hatred for the Jews as the impetus for destruction, his National Socialist German Worker's Party (Nazis) hunted for Jews. Jews who did not escape this madman were left broken in mind, body, and spirit.

Beginning in 1933, and continuing for the twelve years he was in power, Hitler implemented his plan for the "Jewish Problem:" legal disenfranchisement of the Jews to legalized murder. During this reign of terror, fifteen million people were killed, including members of other ethnic groups, especially Gypsies, Poles, Slavs, as well as homosexuals, although the policy aimed at Jews was the most deliberate and well calculated.

Other European countries were beginning to follow Germany's lead in persecuting their minorities. There was almost no opposition to what was happening, even on the part of the churches. There was eager support where centuries of deeply ingrained Christian anti-Semitism erupted under cover of war.

---

[1] The Holocaust: Memories, Research, References: Eds. Robert Hauptman, Susan Hubbs Motin

In the years that followed Hitler's rise to power, Nazi-sponsored propaganda was widely disseminated and Jewish books were burned. Anti-Jewish riots in Germany and Austria included *Kristallnacht* or "Night of the Broken Glass," of November 9-10, 1938, when more than 200 synagogues were demolished; and many more Jewish institutions looted and burned, along with 7,500 Jewish-owned businesses. For forty-eight hours, Nazis wearing regular clothes incited others with cries of "Down with the Jews." Carrying hammers, axes, and grenades, brutal mobs roamed the streets smashing windows of Jewish stores, demolishing and looting Jewish homes, and setting fire to or destroying synagogues. German insurance companies were released from their obligation to cover the damages done to Jewish property. The Jews themselves would have to pay for both the losses they had suffered and the cleanup. This pogrom, with 30,000 Jews arrested and imprisoned, was not the first of such indignities and humiliations suffered by the Jews at the hands of the Germans, but it was certainly the most devastating. A great and long-lived center of Jewish learning had perished; the cultural richness of Jewish life in Eastern Europe was lost forever.

The Germans reenacted *Kristallnacht* in every town they invaded and occupied. All over Poland, synagogues went up in flames. Those spared the fire were desecrated, turned into stables, garages, and public latrines. Everywhere, the Germans ordered pogroms, rounding up the non-Jewish population to witness and learn how to mock, abuse, injure, and murder Jews. In 1939, under cover of World War II, ghettos, slave labor camps, and death camps were created where prisoners were either gassed and then burned in crematoria, or worked to death. Doctors performed cruel experiments on prisoners, adults and children.

The "Final Solution to the Jewish Problem" was planned at the Wannsee Conference in 1942. All Jews were to be evacuated to camps in Eastern Europe. Many were to be killed outright; others would endure slave labor and meager rations until they died of natural means. The Nazis had little trouble recruiting help from among the citizens of other countries to staff the camps. The most numerous, enthusiastic, and energetic helpers of the Nazis in each phase of the death process were from Ukraine, a part of Russia that Hitler occupied.

The Germans kept their actions as secret as possible, to keep the world from knowing, and to deceive their victims in many ways to prevent resistance. After word of the slaughter leaked out to the Jews in Poland, partisan groups fought back in Warsaw, and in other cities, though they were outnumbered and for the most part unarmed. Jews also staged uprisings in several concentration camps, but because of their malnourished condition and circumstances, it did little more than serve to incite and bring harsher punishment from their German captors.

The allies repeatedly refused to attempt any rescue of European Jews. American Jews were warned against seeking special actions for the benefit of European Jewry. Zionists managed to save small groups of young Jews and bring them to Palestine. The churches in Europe and outside were mainly silent, but some clergy and a number of courageous non-Jews took part in saving individual Jewish lives. The Danish people as a whole undertook the most successful and heroic effort, transferring the entire Danish Jewish community to neutral Sweden in private boats, thereby saving them from destruction. When the war ended and allied troops entered Germany and Eastern Europe, news of the Holocaust had a shattering effect upon the world, but especially upon a German public already disheartened by defeat.

W.H.

Introduction

The story I am about to tell is of the downward destruction of Eastern European Jewry during the German occupation of Poland, from 1939-1945, and my own personal recollection of that era.

When the second World War began, I became totally isolated from my previous musical environment. And yet, I managed to covertly sing and conduct services with other slave-labor camp inmates while living under unspeakable conditions. It helped some of us to survive.

I speak of my lost family, of the Cracow Ghetto, of the hardships we faced, of the indomitable spirit of the incarcerated Polish Jews in the camps—of death, of destruction, of life after the camps.

I survived to complete three years of intensive vocal study at the Giuseppe Verdi Conservatory, in Torino, Italy, and quite a few years at the Cantor's Institute of the College of Jewish Studies, in Chicago, Illinois. I was uplifted by the golden era of Hazzanuth in the United States—in the period of J. Rosenblatt, Z. Kwartin, D. Hershman, D. Roitman, and many others—the artistry of their interpretation of the prayers will remain in our musical heritage forever.

To be uplifted by such wonders in the world of music is to me the ultimate survival. And now, my story…

PART I

The Early Years

It was the custom of the townspeople in Cracow to gather around 4:30 on Sunday afternoons at the outdoor cafes of coffeehouses. My parents would take me to one of several such establishments that my father's specialty store supplied with products for the making of gourmet baked goods. Of course, we were always treated royally by the coffeehouse proprietors.

As soon as the music would begin—and there was *always* music—I would climb up on a chair and, using a spoon as my baton, wave my arms exactly to the beat of the music. I was all of four years old. Ah, my parents would say, this child is destined for a life of music. No doubt my musical ability came from my paternal grandfather, a well known Baalei T'Filah[2] and from my own father's love of the violin which he played for family and friends. This was to become the introduction to my life's work.

I am reminded of another tradition, a weekly family reunion that was important to all of my family when I was a child—*havdalah*. At the appearance of the stars each Saturday evening, we would all go to my paternal grandparents' home. My grandmother would bid the Sabbath

---

2 Baalei T' Filah is the person who leads the congregation in prayer-the master of prayer. It was the tradition of the Baalei T' Filah to listen to hazzanim in the big cities and bring new melodies back with him to the shul.

farewell by chanting a beautiful prayer. Then the family—aunts, uncles, cousins—would gather around my grandfather for the *havdalah* ceremony, the lifting of a goblet of wine as he chanted the *havdalah* prayer, pronounced a benediction over the wine, a second benediction while inhaling the spices, and still another thanking the Almighty for creating light. We had thirty Hauben family members, including the children, who were present for this celebration of the end of the Sabbath. If someone didn't show up, everyone wanted to know what happened. After the ceremony, the little children were given small bags filled with candies (toffee was my favorite), nuts, fruits, and perhaps a penny or two in celebration of the end of the Sabbath and the beginning of the workweek. After *havdalah* or sometimes on Sundays, we would all go to the Jewish theater, something my father dearly loved. I remember it very well: the productions of the famous *Dybuk opera, Fiddler on the Roof, Shulamit operetta*.

At age six (1928), with my parents' encouragement, I began singing in the synagogue choirs, as an alto, and became greatly influenced by the sheer beauty of the voices of the guest *hazzanim* brought in for the High Holy Day services to chant the beautiful cantorial renditions of the liturgy. I studied cantorial art under the tutelage of prominent cantors until I became a soloist. I think back to the beauty of this particular period of my life as I read in *The Cantors: Gifted Voices Remembered*, "If a composer were to capture the sound of Jewish life of that time it would arise from the music of the synagogue—music that is remembered with passion and reverence—the music of the great cantorial voices." My life as a youngster was filled with the joy of music.

At the same time that I was introduced to singing in the choir, my beloved brother, Romek (Abraham), came along. We were six years apart in age. Although Romek and I did not resemble each other in appearance or demeanor—my mother (of blessed memory) compared us to Esau and Jacob of the bible—we both knew as we were growing up that we were part of a strong family unit, something instilled in us by two loving parents. The best way for me to describe the differences between Romek and me is to say that he was more of an "outsider," a boy with lots of friends—mostly in the Gentile world. He was a good student, very mature for his age of twelve and looking several years older. The fact that he did not look Jewish proved an advantage during the time the family spent in Cracow Ghetto during the war years. Romek lived outside the ghetto, with Gentile friends, and regularly smuggled in food, money, and other necessities, helping us survive through some difficult times.

For many years, even before I was born, my parents lived in a modest home in the Jewish section of Cracow known as the Kazimierz district. We continued to live there at Waska 12 in a very comfortable two-bedroom apartment on the third floor of a building not far from the "Alte Shul."[3]

My dear father, Solomon, was the oldest of twelve children. He was a pious man, although not the Hasidic Jew my grandfather was. A well-educated man, in his early 40's, my father spoke Polish, Yiddish, Hebrew, and German fluently. He was a modern Jew who believed in being close to Judaism, expecting the same for his sons. My father's superb personality was a great asset in his business dealings with mostly Gentile clientele. He was a very ambitious man, trying always to improve our standard of living. Cheder education for his sons at the prestigious Ivri-Mizrachi, and Gymnasium Tachkemoni Hebrew high schools in Cracow was of great importance to him. Each Friday night, my father would be checking out the bible portion we had learned that week. He would open up the bible, and we would have to translate the

---

[3] The Alte Shul (Old (Stara) Synagogue) was built by the Polish king, Kazimierz the Great, who invited the Jewish people to settle in Poland, and guaranteed their freedom. As a symbol of friendship, he built the famous Shul in the fourteenth century.

commentaries and sermons for him from the original text and tell him what they meant. This was not only customary for children who attended Hebrew school, but compulsory for each child to prove that he had the education, and that the money for education was being well spent. In those years, with such rigorous training, a boy of Bar Mitzvah age was extremely knowledgeable of Torah and what was to be expected of him as he entered manhood. I studied in Aramaic, a Semitic language known from the ninth century B.C. (this is the language that Jesus spoke, a combination of Hebrew and Ladino), the original language of the Talmud. My father would always say, they can never take education away from you.

In Cracow, the Jewish community established a special kitchen for the poor called *Beth Lechem*, the House of Nourishment. The main meal was on the Shabbath day, after the morning services. To get a Shabbath meal, one had to present a special ticket, which had to be bought before the Shabbath day. My father would always purchase tickets, not only for beggars, but also for people of high standards and dignity who were in need of assistance. The ritual director would then collect all tickets from members of the synagogue and distribute them to selected individuals who would not know where the sponsored tickets came from. I remember my mother complaining to my father that he was giving away too much. As far as my father was concerned, he could never do enough for those in need of help. He was a righteous person in his own right.

My father was an importer and distributor of ingredients for baked goods, desserts, and candies. When I was old enough, he would explain the products to me. Sometimes I traveled with him to Austria, Germany, Rumania, Hungary, and Yugoslavia to buy the raw materials: airtight silver containers of aromatic cocoa, vanilla beans, saffron (for egg-like coloring), shredded coconut (my favorite snack), big barrels of kartoffel syrup (for making candies), agar (a Japanese product for making gelatin desserts), and many, many others. The most important product he imported was extracts of all kinds; orange, lemon, rum, chocolate, and almond. It was a team effort—my mother was inside managing the store and business responsibilities while my father was out meeting with customers or traveling to buy the products. I sometimes helped out in the store after school. As busy as she was, my mother always found time to invite guests to our home, especially for festivals and minor religious Holy Days, such as Purim and Hanukah.

My beloved mother, Gertrude, thirty-nine at the time, was a kind, loving, and generous person. Her nickname—"Eyshet Chayil"—a woman of valor, was well earned. I remember it so well from my childhood; how extremely busy my mother was with a half dozen organizations. She was especially involved with the Jewish National Fund (JNF, the reforesting agent in Israel) distributing and collecting the little blue boxes. A naturally gifted speaker, in 1936 my mother was elected to a position of JNF vice president for the Cracow region. Many meetings took place in our apartment at Waska 12. The meetings were usually held on Sunday afternoons, with amateur entertainment—my father would play the violin, while one of the members played the piano and helped out with vocal production. We sang mostly Israeli songs; it was uplifting. We envisioned that sometime in the near future there would be a country we could call our own—the country we now call the State of Israel. My mother's group started out small, maybe ten to fifteen members. Just before the beginning of World War II, the organization grew to fifty members.

A native of Cracow, my mother was born into a prominent, well-to-do, and highly regarded family. There were two daughters, Gertrude and Malia; and two sons, Simon and Herman. When both sons were old enough, they helped with the business, a wholesale import operation specializing in fresh fruits, as well as other products not available in Poland. Oranges, lemons, grapefruit, bananas, coconuts, peaches, grapes, and almonds were among the products they imported for distribution in Poland. Later, they expanded their business to include dried fruits and sardines from France, Portugal, and Spain. When my parents married, my grandfather gave my father his first business location to start his own importing operation.

* * * *

My musical studies continued and, at the age of fifteen, after my voice had changed, my father said, "Now, you are a tenor." My formal music education was to begin with training in both piano and voice. Further studies in opera and the cantorate enabled me to sing the music of the great composers, as well as intricate Hebraic chants.

Life came to a stop as the German forces crossed into Poland in the early hours of Friday, September 1, 1939. This date marked the beginning of World War II and unimaginable horrors perpetrated against the Jews in German-occupied Europe. (Poland suffered some of the war's heaviest casualties, losing six million people and 40 percent of its national wealth).

German Occupation—1939-1940

We could hear the sound of heavy artillery in the distance; ten to twenty miles from Cracow. The German forces had defeated the Polish army in two weeks. The fighting did not reach our beautiful city of Cracow[4], and by a stroke of good fortune, and little resistance by the Polish army, our historic buildings monuments, and museums survived unharmed.

---

[4] Cracow is an ancient, historic city built in the Middle Ages. The center of the city has remained largely unchanged. The Royal Castle, once the home of Poland's kings, is filled with important collections of tapestries and paintings.

At first the German army gained a foothold in Cracow by crossing over two bridges at the perimeter of the city. A motorcycle brigade took the lead, binoculars poised, searching the rooftops for snipers. Troops followed on horseback carrying supplies. There was no shooting at this time, simply a quiet acquisition of our town and citizenry—the taking of a city. Little did we realize that life for Jews in Cracow would never be the same.

The dehumanizing first blow to the entire Jewish population of Cracow began after several months of German occupation. The SS High Command took over the administration of the local government, and the beginning of Jewish persecution started. First, our rations for food were restricted to starvation rations, less than half of non-Jewish Polish citizens. All Jewish people had to register with the SS to perform duties such as snow removal, street cleaning, and collection of garbage. It was "forced labor," and only Jews employed by the German Wehrmacht (army) authorities were exempt: those performing domestic labor, or municipal workers employed by the Germans.

In 1939, as part of the forced slave labor edict, I was assigned to the Polish Mienkina, a stone crushing operation in a suburb of Cracow. I crushed stones for a period of eight months. As I reflect on the contrast of my life as a seventeen-year-old adolescent immersed in the study of music and Torah with that of a slave laborer, crushing rocks into stones, I wonder how I survived the ordeal. We survived by doing as we were told. Perhaps the discipline of my early training was the necessary preparation for what my life was to become under Nazi rule. In any event, I simply followed orders. There was no other choice.

Dynamite was used to blow up rock formation at the stone mine. My job was to break apart the large stones and crush them with a hammer called a "stone mill." We worked out of doors and it was all very primitive. The crushed stones were used by a German company to build roads. The Germans began improving the Polish roads and highways for their own purposes, using the Jewish workers who were obligated to provide the necessary raw material of crushed stone. When we finished crushing our allotment of stones, we loaded it all onto wagons, and then pushed the heavy load to the road where trucks were waiting for us to once again do the loading. It was grueling manual labor for all of the Jewish workers. We were like mules being driven by harsh, unmerciful masters.

I worked on this stone-crushing project five days a week. Barracks provided as my living quarters by the company made it a fairly comfortable living arrangement for me. I was supervised by a Polish engineer in charge of production who was directly supervised by the German authorities. One weekend I decided to take some time off to be with my family and didn't report for required roll call. Upon my return to work, I was arrested and taken to a temporary prison located in a former Polish elementary school in Cracow.

As far as I can remember, the first basic policy of the Germans was the systematic removal of anyone with opinions, or an opposing point of view, especially the "intelligentsia." I was interrogated by a team of SS officers (the SS wore on their uniforms the death head emblem—a skull and crossbones—to signify that they were as obedient as corpses to their leaders). They demanded the names of former teachers and principals (both Polish and Jewish) and their affiliations in political clubs and activities. This was early 1940, a time when ghettos and concentration camps did not yet exist.

After three days under lock and key, with fairly mild questioning, the situation changed considerably. The SS officers returned and said they were prepared to execute my entire family if I did not tell them of people known to me who were against the Hitler administration. My answer was simple and truthful. I knew a number of individuals, mostly in areas of Poland other than Cracow where there had been heavy fighting and loss of life. These people were lost in the battle and did not return from war.

It was obvious that my response to their questioning did not satisfy them. At this point, they put tremendous pressure on me, reducing my food to one bowl of soup daily, and black imitation (ersatz) coffee. After a few more days of this treatment, a new team of SS officers arrived. They asked, among other things, of my family's activities, and whether I was personally involved with any political organizations. I told them that Akiva, the Zionist youth group (named after the legendary Rabbi Akiva Ben Joseph, scholar of the Mishna), was the only organization of which I was a member. The interrogation was conducted in the German language without an interpreter. After a few more hours of further questioning, and intimidation, I was released. My good luck was that I had an employment certificate (work card) from the Polish Mienkina, proof positive that I was employed with papers recognized by the German authorities. I could walk freely in the streets without fear and the threat of harassment by the Germans, who could easily have rounded me up and assigned me to an even more tedious work detail than the Polish Mienkina stone crushing operation.

Later in 1940, it was mandated that every able-bodied man register for forced labor in the nearby former Polish military airport. Because of my experience, (I learned the trade as an apprentice, helping my cousin, Zyga Riegelhaupt, to carry the tools and hand equipment to the electricians), I was assigned to install electrical cables, which I did for about twenty months. The Kabel Company and two other companies—Artur Johr Company and the Oscar Riedel Company—were in charge of work on the electrical cables, private German ownership serving the Luftwaffe (German Air Force). There were three groups of workers. The first group was digging six to fifteen inches below the ground to make room for the cables. The second group laid down the cable. The third group, of which I was a part, put electrical wires and switch connections together.

During this period, my maternal grandparents, Marcus and Hadassah Grunwald, lived in a mixed neighborhood close to the Jewish district in Cracow. As *native* Slovakian citizens, they enjoyed the privileges of foreign citizens in occupied Poland (suffered none of the degradation of Polish Jews). Their status was honored and respected by the German authorities, although every foreign citizen had to be registered by the German administration. Proof of legitimate foreign documents had to be witnessed. After investigating the documents with each of the foreign consulates, the German authority then declared that a special label with name, country of origin, and the flag of their native country be placed in the front entrance of the apartment they occupied. It was the responsibility of each foreign citizen to have his own label made to these specifications. Fortunately for my family, we were able to spend a couple of months at my grandparents' home, while the Cracow Ghetto was in its formative stages in early 1941. We were being forced to evacuate to the suburbs because of our lack of proper credentials to enter the ghetto.

SS Units Search For The Valuables

In 1940, as my family sat in the living room one summer evening, we heard a commotion outside. There was heavy shooting in the streets, throughout the entire district. We watched as the SS military units encircled the neighborhood, while large military trucks passed through the streets. They were conducting a search in an effort to loot our valuables—gold, silver, jewelry, American dollars, and objects of art. It was a nightmare for everyone, especially the little children who did not know what would come next. We were forced to remain inside for three days and nights.

The real drama took place on the second day of the encirclement. There was a loud knock at our door at the wee hours of the morning. A middle-aged German police officer of the Shutz Polizei Unit shouted, "Machen sie auf" (Open the door"). He was of the Order Police (ORPO), units used to roundup or kill Jews. Removing his helmet and putting his gun on the table in our dining room, he made himself comfortable. "I assume you are intelligent people, and you would understand what we came for," he said. He ordered us to put our rings, gold, and other personal jewelry in a large dish. Within five minutes we were also to place everything else of value on the table. He said that if we didn't fulfill his orders, we would "be shot on the spot." As instructed, we delivered our silver menorah, two silver Shabbat candlesticks, a gorgeous museum piece candelabra, all our silver, copper and bronze. He seemed pleased with our cooperation.

We were then to carry all our valuables down from the third floor to be loaded onto a waiting truck. We could hear people from other apartments being beaten, so we considered ourselves lucky.

In the middle of the second night, four SS soldiers kicked in our door. They broke in like crazed baboons, telling us that this was the "real" search for valuables. My mother became distraught, and angry. She was beaten badly. The men didn't touch my father, my brother, or me. We were wearing special badges, having earlier worked for and loaded the trucks for the special police unit. The soldiers meticulously searched our books looking for hidden money. A few hours later, another group of SS men came, and the search turned into frenzied activity. They turned the entire apartment upside down, throwing everything on the floor, especially the books, leaving our home in shambles.

Still later that night another group of SS soldiers arrived. They turned over furniture and searched pockets of all our clothing. In the streets, other SS units celebrated by opening fire, shooting directly into the windows of apartments. They had been ordered to demoralize and degrade the Jews in the Kazimierz district; they succeeded.

Mandates and the Dilemma of Evacuation to the Ghetto

During this period in 1939-1941, before the establishment of the ghetto, the entire Jewish population of Cracow faced incredibly harsh orders from the German administration. The official records of the Polish War Crimes Tribunal reported the following mandates for persecution of the Jews by the Nazi administration: It was mandated by order on August 9, 1939, that all Jewish businesses be marked by the Star of

David; this led to plundering of the establishments and persecution of the owners and managers. Soon after, on October 10, 1939, Governor Hans Frank issued a proclamation that stated that in the lands governed by the Germans there would be no room for the Jews, the exploiters (more than 10,000 Jews from the countryside arrived in Cracow daily, as per mandated orders). On this same date, Hans Frank introduced forced labor for the Jewish population by forming labor groups, and the carrying out of that order was given to his deputy for matters of security, the chief SS and the police chief.

From November 1939 on the security police known as the Gestapo mandated that all Jewish deposits, ledgers and accounts be frozen. From December 1939 Jews could only be seen on the streets if wearing a band with a Star of David on the right arm, with restriction as to when they were permitted to be on the streets. Shortly after, it was mandated that Jews were not allowed to travel by rail, and that Jewish schools were banned until September 1940, after which the Jewish Council was given the task of administering Jewish education. The Jewish Council was comprised of twenty-four elected Jews personally responsible for carrying out the regime (Nazi's orders) in Cracow, such as making up lists for work detail, and dividing of food and housing. It was also a place to lodge complaints. From January 1, 1940, Jews were not allowed to move without a special permit.[5] The Jewish population was saddled with the demeaning tasks of collecting garbage, removing snow, and cleaning public roads.

---

[5] When uncertain if a man was a Jew, the Germans checked to see if he was circumcised. A distinguished plastic surgeon had taught a number of young Cracow Jews how to lengthen their foreskins bloodlessly, by sleeping with a weight—a bottle containing a gradually increasing volume of water—attached to themselves. It was a device used by Jews in periods of Roman persecution, and this surgeon revived its use to help the young men to survive.

The Germans began to block off certain Jewish neighborhoods in Cracow, and apartments lived in by Jewish people had to be abandoned and closed by a specific date, with keys delivered to the German trust officer. The restrictions went on and on in a never-ending spiral of degradation and contempt for the Jewish population including a restrictive edict forbidding the kosher preparation of meat.

The activity within the district of Cracow was only one fragment of a wider action whose goal was the extermination of the Jewish population of Europe, which was carried out in steps. First was the economic and personal deprivation, followed by the loss of personal liberty in the form of confinement in the so-called ghettos. From there the people were moved to concentration camps and finally mass murdered through shooting and gassing.

* * * *

The Jewish ghetto in Cracow was created in the spring of 1941. Edict 44/91 established a closed Jewish district south of the Vistula River in the Cracow suburb of Podgórze. Jews in Cracow were forced from their homes and required to crowd into an area of only sixteen square blocks, in isolation from other non-Jewish Polish citizens, and surrounded by barbed wire and walls. Before the war, Cracow had a population of 56,000 Jews from all walks of life: professionals, educators, blue collar workers. Charity was very common; the very rich always helped the poor (anti-Semitism had always been a problem for the Jews in Poland). The Jewish population swelled to 68,000 as Jews in the neighboring small towns and villages fled to the big city, as the Germans began to direct the flow of human traffic that soon radically altered the age-old pattern of Jewish settlement in Poland. The Jews were uprooted from 16,000 ancient Jewish communities and sent to the big cities. Some 330,000 Jews, one tenth of the Jews in Poland, became homeless refugees, beggars of bread and shelter, candidates for disease and death. Forlorn and friendless, in strange big cities, the refugees were thrust into the inadequate mercies of communities already burdened with their own wants.

Another edict, a sedative clause, promised to protect the Jews from their Polish countrymen. There were pogroms against the Jewish population beginning in 1935. Jewish industries were starved under new laws on bank credit. Craft guilds were closed to Jewish artisans; universities introduced a quota on the entry of Jewish students. In the first days of the German occupation, the conquerors had been astonished by the willingness of Poles to point out Jewish households. In March 1941, the promise to protect the ghetto dwellers from Polish national excess fell on the ear most credibly. The Jews of Cracow had a sense that they wouldn't be uprooted or tyrannized when they moved to the Cracow Ghetto.

When Cracow was designated the capital of the *Generalgovernement* by Governor Hans Frank, he ordered the voluntary departure of all Jews, except for those "economically indispensable." Very few refugees complied. After three months, the Germans took matter into their own hands and expelled 32,000 Jews from Cracow. My family was part of this mass exodus to the suburbs, as we did not have the necessary Kennkarte (work card) to move into the Cracow Ghetto.

The deadline for moving into the ghetto was March 20, 1941, for those who qualified. All others had to leave Cracow, which was now proclaimed as *judenrein* (free of Jews). There was incredible chaos and panic in the Jewish neighborhoods at this time. Everyone was preparing for evacuation to the suburban areas. Because of all the delays by the Polish authorities, it was at this point that my family moved in with my grandparents for several months, before relocating to Gorka Narodowa Village. Having this temporary relief was a blessing at this time of crisis in my life. It was not until one year later that we received approval from the German administration to move into the Cracow Ghetto. While preparing for our move to the ghetto, we received unsettling news about the conditions there: lack of living accommodations, fear of arrest, severe hunger, poor medical treatment and facilities. It was frightening for our family, although the propaganda from the Germans would lead people to believe otherwise.

Life in the Cracow Ghetto

Jews who entered the Cracow Ghetto were met with a fancy wooden gate that looked something like the Ten Commandments gracing the front entrance. The wide arches allowed the trolleys to pass through (the Cracow trolley continued its route coming and going from Cracow, which happened to be directly through the center of the ghetto. Barbed wire and brick walls enclosed it, and, although ghetto dwellers were not permitted to use it, they were sometimes able to hop on when guards were looking the other way). Above the arches a sign designated the Cracow Ghetto as "Jewish Town," to reassure newcomers that they were welcome and in a secure place. High barbed wire fences had been strung along the front of the ghetto facing the Vistula River, while nine-foot tombstone-like pillars filled in the open spaces, with brick walls enclosing the entire ghetto.

There were three entrances to the Cracow Ghetto. The main entrance, guarded by two German soldiers, was used to maintain order. The side entrance, guarded by Polish police, was located at the Platz Zgody (Square of Agreement) and was used primarily by people going to their places of employment or returning. The Germans and Polish police used this checkpoint to examine documents carried by the workers passing through the gate, and it was the gate through which official business was conducted. Thousands of people passed through the gates to their jobs in the city. The gates were locked at night.

We were all aware that smuggling was taking place, mostly through the rear (third) entrance of the ghetto guarded by Polish police. Smuggling was our only means of survival, as hunger was pervasive throughout the ghetto. Bartering for food was often accomplished by workers employed outside the ghetto using clothing or household goods as a medium of exchange. The ghetto police often permitted contraband food to come in. Bribery sometimes induced leniency. Surprisingly, children were often our most successful smugglers. They were small and agile and could move in and out of the ghetto undetected. On occasion, if caught, they were often a subject of pity for the policeman.[6] Although smuggling was demoralizing, it kept most Jews from dying of hunger.

Guards with rifles and machine guns stood posted at all ghetto openings, ready to obey the law, which stated:

Jews who leave without authorization will be punished by death.

The same punishment applies to persons who knowingly provide
a hiding place for Jews or things Jewish.

The high brick walls were an ominous presence for those of us contained within. Christians lived on the other side of the wall—free. Jews lived inside as prisoners. Streets were dirty and houses were rundown. Families unknown to one another lived ten to twelve in a small two-room apartment. In winter there was little heat. Keeping clean and having enough water were problems throughout the year. Pipes and plumbing fixtures that broke down were not fixed again. There were pharmacies with no drugs to sell. Many stores stood empty, looted by German and Polish police. Private homes had been turned into hospitals. These, along with old-age homes and orphanages, were full to overflowing. Signs of poverty were everywhere. Most people walked about in rags. Hunger was the scourge of every ghetto.

---

[6] *The War Against the Jews* by Lucy S. Dawidowicz

Jews received starvation rations. The rations were deliberate. It was the Nazi policy to kill as many Jews as possible by natural means. And one of the means was starvation. Corpses littered the streets. Undertakers went about with hand-drawn or horse-drawn carts collecting corpses and taking them away for burial. Jews were in rags because they had to sell off whatever they owned to buy food. When they had nothing more to sell, they took to the streets with tin cups, begging.

The ghetto Jews lived in such cramped quarters that normal conventions of privacy or modesty were soon forgotten. There was little sense of shame, which perhaps in a sense may have helped to prepare the Jews for what was yet to come, the untold indignities we were to endure as inmates at the hands of the Germans. Rather than share a tiny two-room apartment with strangers, many ghetto residents chose to live with extended family members. At least it was family.

With so many people crowded together in such close proximity, there could be heard in the streets a deafening clamor of voices, and cries of people dying on the sidewalk who just happened to be in the wrong place when German police appeared for a roundup to fill their daily quota of Jews to be transferred out of the ghetto. The fetid odor of latrines was everywhere, toilets beyond repair poisoning the air with an ominous, gaseous smell.

Staying warm in winter was the highest priority. Assuming there was fuel available, ghetto dwellers had to decide if it was to be used to cook the family's main meal, for heat, or to bathe one's self and family. All necessities in the normal course of living were now reduced to a choice of what the family could do without.

For centuries, Jews have shared a deep faith in ultimate survival, preservation, and continuity of Jewish life. Most Jews in the ghetto felt this great sense of community, of belonging. Family relationships prospered in times of stress, became the stronghold, the source of comfort and moral strength—protecting the family, educating the children, feeding the hungry, and caring for the sick. They shared their hopes and plans, and assumed responsibility for extended family members—grandparents, aunts, uncles, siblings—the young helping the old, parents and children dividing responsibility. Tenderness and affection replaced passion; the ghetto heightened emotional needs of all family members.

The ghetto children were sheltered in legal or underground schools that provided warmth, medical and sanitary care, food, and emotional security. It was a subcommunity of love and dedication, with invisible walls protecting them against ghetto harshness and ugliness. For the children this was a tiny oasis of joy and creativity in the bleakness of ghetto life (for the adults, there were underground circulating libraries, concerts, and music that was sometimes brought into the homes and apartments by outside entertainers).

In Cracow Ghetto, thousands of children received traditional instruction in Judaism privately, or in secret schools. The Germans had excluded Jewish children from public schools, intending to deprive them of education. They underestimated the place of education in the system of Jewish values.

The welfare of the children drove people into despair. Nazis were taking the children away and no one knew where. Some people gave their children to Christian families for safekeeping, or put them in the care of a church or monastery. Parents no longer had safe homes for their children. Children no longer had a childhood. Many children in the ghettos became orphans, many under the age of fifteen. Their parents had been sent to labor camps or had been murdered. In 1946, after the war ended, The United Nations Relief & Rehabilitation Agency learned that the Nazis had stolen hundreds of thousands of fair-haired, blue-eyed non-Jewish Polish children from their homes and sorted them into two categories: "racially valuable" and "worthless." The children who did not meet their stringent requirements, on the basis of measurements of sixty-two parts of their bodies, were returned to their families. To replenish Germany's population, the racially valuable—approximately 250,000—were either placed for adoption with German families for

"Germanization," or in the case of the older boys, were sent away to boarding schools for reeducation.

By 1942 small fortunes in Jewish Joint Distribution Committee cash were handed to trusted contacts in Poland to help people in the Cracow Ghetto. A Budapest jeweler was used to pipe Istanbul rescue money into the German empire through Oskar Schindler for distribution to his contacts in the Jewish community.

This funding for the Jews in the ghetto helped them to follow their natural ingenuity in setting up traditional Jewish trades to support their families. They adhered to Talmud law, which says, "Be pliable like a reed, not rigid like a cedar." They manufactured goods for sale, sometimes in cooperatives in conjunction with ORT, the Jewish agency for vocational training and rehabilitation. They marketed inside and smuggled outside the ghetto legally and illegally—making something out of nothing—producing and preparing food. They manufactured such items as men's and women's clothing, shoes, hats, brushes, and baked goods (bread baking was the key industry in ghettos). The income provided a minimal livelihood for thousands of ghetto residents, although there was heavy taxation on money earned by ghetto industries (many of these industries were moved into Plaszow camp when Cracow Ghetto was liquidated).

Traditional Judaism was forced underground throughout the ghettos. Jews prayed in secret—in cellars, attics, behind closed doors with men on guard. In Cracow Ghetto, services were held in two prayer houses and, with the cooperation of the Jewish policemen who worshiped there, members were kept informed if German police were expected in the area. The survival of the Jews and Judaism depended on

---

[7] *The War Against the Jews* by Lucy S. Dawidowicz

the uninterrupted transmittal of the tradition from generation to generation. Like bread and potatoes, education and culture sustained life in the ghettos.[7]

Underground groups sprang up in all major ghettos. Its members in the ghettos were prisoners, so they were limited in what they could do. Reprisals by the Nazis were severe. For every revolt by the Jews, hundreds of thousands of Jews were liquidated. The underground groups from the ghettos did what they could to destroy or damage German military installations; to find out what Germans were planning for their own or another ghetto; to create underground tunnels as secret exits and secret hiding places; to get underground newspapers into circulation. Members of the Cracow Ghetto dressed in stolen SS uniforms and left a bomb behind in an SS restaurant. The restaurant was blown up. Weapons were smuggled into ghettos. Passport photographs were smuggled out of the ghettos to centers where they could be used in the forging of Aryan papers to arrange for false documents (identity cards) for any who might escape. The underground also acted as a court—Jews accused of collaboration with the Germans were tried and executed.

In addition to underground groups, there were underworld operators who learned of furs withheld from the Germans, contraband goods, forbidden activities, radios, and so on. These blackmailers were despised by the Jewish community. Since personal property and occupation determined class in the ghetto, both of which could buy food and security, the blackmailers knew exactly who their targets were.

Gorka Narodowa Village

The distance from Cracow to the suburbs was about one hour by streetcar. The front of the streetcars was reserved for non-Jews, and the rear was for Jewish people only. While living in the little suburban village of Gorka Narodowa, before we were admitted to Cracow Ghetto, I registered for forced labor at the Polish military airport, Rakowice

Czyzyny. Fortunately, at age nineteen, I was qualified for underground electrical cable work. Our foreman, a Polish engineer named Twarug, was completely in charge of directing the entire group of twenty-five Jewish men for the Kabel company. He was a good man and we were treated nicely. We were paid by the private German company, although the wages didn't amount to much, it was usually enough to live on for a day or two. For lunch, non-German employees got German potato soup, some meat, bread, and margarine. An occasional apple was a bonus. With time, things only got worse. In the summer of 1943, it was reported that sixteen people at the Kabel company were relocated to Plaszow camp and killed by Amon Geoth, commandant at Plaszow.

As Jewish employees, we were all required to wear a blue and white Magen David (Jewish star) on our right arm, so that we could more easily be recognized by the airport police. The employees had to walk in groups of ten people or more. Interestingly enough, we worked without guards. Because we were under the supervision of the Luftwaffe, the SS (Schutzstaffel security squad) was not involved at this time.

During this period, my uncle Simon Grunwald, his wife, Regina, and my cousin, Samy, were living outside the ghetto posing as Gentiles and Hungarian citizens. They had somehow acquired false papers from a dead person. Before our move to the ghetto, a few valuables we had hidden from the Germans were transferred and entrusted to my aunt Regina who sold some of the jewelry to buy us food.

Righteous Persons and the Cracow Ghetto

When we finally received our assignment for an apartment in the ghetto, it was necessary to register with the Jewish administration there (my brother Romek helped to find transportation to move the family to the ghetto; he was always very resourceful). While we were waiting for processing, we were divided, and each of us placed with a different family of strangers in extremely cramped living conditions. Needless to say, we all felt very insecure and uncertain about the future. This was the spring of 1942 and Romek was fourteen years old. Even after our family was reunited Romek was unhappy in the ghetto and the tiny apartment we shared with cousins. He vowed to run away to live outside the ghetto with Gentile friends. We were all so upset and fearful, but there was nothing we could do to stop him. Romek was not afraid to take a risk to help the family or himself. It was a gamble and he knew it, but for him anything was better than the ghetto.

As it turned out, Romek's leaving was a blessing in disguise. He was able to visit us every five days or so smuggling in precious food and communication from the outside world. He had a secret location, and could enter the ghetto at special times. He used a bicycle for transportation and traveled mostly under cover of darkness. Having no identification papers, he dressed as a scout and carried the books of a schoolboy to deceive the Germans. Thanks to my dear brother, we always had enough bread and other necessities in the ghetto. We were moved seven or eight times during our seven-month stay in the ghetto, but Romek always managed to find us. As people were deported to slave labor camps, the ghetto became smaller and smaller as the Germans tightened the boundaries. Survival was all we could think of and, after a while, we felt nothing as the horror of our reality set in.

Of course we had many cousins, aunts, and uncles in the ghetto. My cousin Zyga was a little younger than I was. We were good friends. Before the ghetto, we played soccer together. He had always encouraged me to have a trade. As a master electrician, as we grew older, he helped me a great deal to develop the skills of the trade. By coincidence, we later worked together in shifts at Plaszow Concentration Camp.

The majority of my father's bakery clientele before the German occupation were listed, "organized" Gentiles (registered with the German authority). Prior to moving to the ghetto, we knew our merchandise would eventually be taken away, so we transferred our entire inventory to gourmet bakery locations owned by my father's clients who were Righteous Gentiles.[8] My brother knew the location of these wonderful people and they, in exchange for our merchandise, provided us with precious food we needed to survive. The chairman of the bakery union was Polish, a converted Volksdeutsche (a Polish citizen whose life situation was elevated and improved by virtue of his German descent, and loyalty to Hitler). His name was Jerry Urbanke, a Polish Catholic of German descent. My father spoke German fluently, so they had always been able to converse in German (a way to keep the Polish employees from overhearing their private talk). Jerry Urbanke's relationship with my father was genuine and cordial, and he proved himself to be very trustworthy. His payments were always on time. We never used his name in our conversations, but referred to him as the "Tzaddik" (the Righteous) for our own and his protection. He supplied us with food and money—dry foods, bread, apples, pears, and potatoes (nothing cooked with an aroma that could be detected and attract attention), through the darkest days of the Cracow Ghetto. The little money he gave us was used to bribe a Polish policeman so he wouldn't take milk away from us in the street.

Jerry Urbanke's wife, Helen, also converted from Polish citizenship to become a Volksdeutsche, was a true woman of valor. Because of her permanent status as a supervisor of the ghetto hospital pharmacy, she

---

[8] A Righteous Person—this title is a peculiarly Israeli honor based on an ancient tribal assumption that in the mass of Gentiles, the G-d of Israel would always provide a leavening of just men. Avenue of Righteous Gentiles is located at Yad Vashem Museum located on Mount Remembrance in Jerusalem. It is a tree-lined walk with a tree planted in the name of each Christian who risked his or her life to save Jews. In 1989, about 8,000 of the "Righteous Gentiles Amongst the Nations," a term of honor used by Yad Vashem, were recognized by Israel with a planting of a tree in each of their names along the Yad Vashem Memorial Hall. Yad Vashem is a permanent monument to those who perished—a monument to a nation's grief that commemorates the greatest tragedy in Jewish history—the Holocaust.

visited with us often, sometimes weekly. She brought small packages of food each time, but never on the same day of the week, so as not to arouse suspicion. She also brought medications that were no longer available at the ghetto pharmacy. Because she was trusted by the German authority she was quickly promoted to the director of operation of the hospital pharmacy. We later discovered that she was totally devoted to the cause, and was secretly providing urgently needed medications to the entire Cracow Ghetto population. Helen Urbanke saved many hundreds of Jewish souls. She and her husband were a beacon of light for us and maybe the only Volksdeutsche couple to risk their own lives for a Jewish cause in the darkness of the ghetto. Thank you G-d, for the miracle of human kindness.

My aunt Regina delivered packages to us through my other aunt Regina (Hendel), which contained dry foods, and medicines if needed. Regina Hendel was employed by the famous Madritsch uniform company, which produced uniforms for the German army and employed 4,000 prisoners inside Plaszow camp (Julius Madritsch was a kind man who was concerned about the welfare of his factory workers; he provided them with nourishing soup and good treatment). Madritsch had another location outside the camp where my aunt Regina worked. When I was relocated permanently as a prisoner at Plaszow, I required surgery for my hand. My aunt was able to bring me vital medication, not available in the Plaszow camp hospital.

Ghetto A and Ghetto B

To avoid deportation from the ghetto to the concentration camps, one had to be looking healthy and able-bodied, between twenty and forty years of age, and have a profession or trade that appealed to the German authorities. In the fall of 1942, the Cracow Ghetto was divided into two parts, Ghetto A and Ghetto B. Barbed wire separated the two sections of the ghetto. Ghetto A was for the working people, Ghetto B for the unemployed, elderly, women, children and sick people not qualified to work. I registered myself as an electrician. In the meantime, there were rumors that both parts of the ghetto were to be liquidated. From ghetto sources and the Polish underground (paid by the Jews for information about Jewish deportation by the Germans), we learned deportation meant almost certain death.

In the last quarter of 1942, the Germans began to build a larger camp in Plaszow. Up until this time, Plaszow had been a smaller working camp, from where Jews were transported to work in various German firms. The new Plaszow camp was supervised by SS Oberscharfuhrer (sergeant) Muller, construction supervisor (Amon Goeth was Muller's chief aide, then became the infamous commandant of the new camp). The special workers from Ghetto A (plumbers, electricians, upholsterers, carpenters, painters, shoemakers, tailors, and mechanics of all sorts) were assigned to build the new Plaszow camp, which was divided into five main parts: the watch block, Jewish barracks, administration buildings, industrial buildings, and what was to be the mass graves beyond the barbed wire fences. My selection as a special worker at Plaszow was protection from being deported to other forced labor camps. I was then twenty years old. As a qualified electrician, I lived outside the camp at first, but was later imprisoned during the October *Aktion* that separated me from my parents and brother.

Romek was dong well outside the ghetto. He never stayed with us overnight, because it was too dangerous without identification papers. However, during the week of October 28, 1942, he came down with a high fever and stayed with us for a few days to recover. Unfortunately, this happened to be the week of another barbaric deportation of 7,000 more Jews sent to the liquidation camps. The selection process was relatively simple. We lined up and the officer in charge would nod his head this way and that, indicating the direction for those of us who were to stay, and those of us who were to go. The criteria were: Are you qualified to work? Are you the right age? Are you healthy? If not, we don't need you. My parents and brother were among the unfortunate ones selected to be deported to the infamous death camp of destruction—Belzec.

They met none of the criteria and I never heard from them again. I was in shock, devastated beyond belief, as were others who lost their loved ones. May their souls be bound up in blessed memory.

October *Aktion* on Platz Zgody

The particular October 28, 1942 *Aktion* (rounding up of Jews to be transported out of the ghetto to forced labor camps, or machine-gunned on the spot) that separated me from my parents was conducted by a Sturmbandfuhrer (a high ranking SS officer) named Willi Haase. It took place at Platz Zgody, the square in Cracow Ghetto. Haase was the most brutal and scientifically inclined *Aktion* expert up to this date. As I watched my parents and brother directed one way, I suddenly found myself directed toward a group of 500-1000 people, all waiting as "reserve cargo." We were to be deported with the transport if the partic- ular quota was not achieved. When quotas were not met, people of all ages were selected at random for the transports out of the ghetto. Selections were made at the whim of the German officer in charge. It was heartbreaking to see families broken up, children torn from their mothers' arms and husbands separated from their wives and children. It was not unusual for a band to be playing peppy children's songs as the children were led away, often without their mothers. We were rounded up by a special unit of Sonderdienst soldiers (Special Action Unit Guard). The waiting time was unbelievably torturous. . .like waiting at death's door. We were like chickens, trapped behind chicken wire. Miraculously, after a few hours of waiting, an order came from the SS officer in charge that we were temporarily free, and we were released. I went home reciting the Ha'Gomel prayer thanking the Almighty for saving my soul from certain death:

Praised are you, Lord our G-d, King of the Universe
who graciously bestows favor upon the undeserving, even
as he has bestowed favor upon me.

By this time, the situation in Cracow Ghetto had deteriorated to such
an extent that signs of poverty were everywhere. People who had sold
everything begged for food, with children standing by their side. It was
wartime and food for everyone inside and outside the ghetto was scarce.
German authorities let it be known that the starvation food rations for
Jews was for a "population which does no work worth mentioning."

Evacuation to Plaszow Forced Labor Camp

Soon after the October *Aktion,* I was transferred as an inmate to the
nearby Zwansarbeislager (forced labor camp) in Cracow-Plaszow, to
face the number one expert and brutal murderer, Amon Goeth, who
was to become the camp commandant. Plaszow was known as the most
notorious forced labor camp in Poland, from October 26, 1942 to
September 13, 1944. After the war Amon Goeth was arrested at an SS
sanatorium at Bad Tolz. He was convicted and hanged by order of the
Polish War Crimes Tribunal in 1946, at age thirty-eight. He went to the
gallows without remorse giving the National Socialist salute before
dying. He was accused of immediate complicity in mass genocide, as
being one of the ideological pioneers in carrying out the criminal procedures of extermination. Goeth was formally arrested by the SS on
September 13, 1944, on charges of taking valuables, furniture, and other
personal property from victims in the ghetto and camps for his own
personal use. From whatever was found and confiscated, only a small
portion was forwarded to the German government; the rest of it he kept
for himself. He was also charged with misuse of the camp's resources, in
particular stealing meat, flour, and other foods for his own use and

resale. Goeth escaped from the German prison where he was placed. He was later captured by Americans shortly after Germany collapsed.

* * *

I was registered as an electrician assigned to the electrical group directed by the Jewish kapo named Mahauf. The kapo was a prisoner foreman. The kapos were frequently drawn from the criminal element. Some used their power to help prisoners; many used it for personal gain. They had power of life and death over prisoners, and in many instances beat and clubbed prisoners to death. A group of German prisoners became kapos after Plaszow became a concentration camp—sadistic, warped criminals controlled the inmates' lives.

My duties in the group also included maintenance of the camp barracks (as was the case with most inmates, I was assigned to fill in on other work details). As I made my way around the camp, I learned that Plaszow was built on top of a new Jewish cemetery. The Germans had shattered gravestones from the grave sites to build the road that ran the length of Plaszow, splitting it in two. The old cemetery was adjacent to the hilly dunes of the new cemetery.

The Ukrainian Guard barracks were almost ready for occupation, except for the electrical installation. Half of our team of twenty electricians was assigned to installing electricity in these barracks as soon as possible. While working in one of the barracks, I met a Ukrainian guard who said he was an accomplished accordionist and superb musician. He told me that he had heard from the kitchen help that I had a fine singing voice. When I was hungry, which was more often than not, I would go to the kitchen and sing for the kitchen help; in turn they would give me food. He was exceptionally nice to me, bringing a bowl of hot soup for me to the barracks where I was working. I later discovered that he was an important member of the entertainment group. He spoke Polish, Russian, and German fluently. He said he needed a man who understood music, and asked if I would look at some Russian and German music. I told him that I came from a musical family, that my mother played the piano and my father the violin, and that I would be pleased to participate in the group's entertainment. I was scared, but felt that my survival was at stake.

One day when the guard was on duty, he came to my barracks and asked if I would be able to provide some popular or classical renditions for the entertainment group. I later learned that women were strictly prohibited from participation in or entertaining the Ukrainian Guard. To fraternize with or touch a Jewish girl was not permitted. (A brothel for the convenience of the Ukrainians and German soldiers and guards was permitted, staffed by girls who had been chosen, or had volunteered, from among the Polish inmates who were interred in the camp).

A guard picked me up one Sunday morning and took me to meet Igor, the leader of the entertainment group. Igor was eagerly waiting in his office for me, along with a sergeant of the Ukrainian Guard. The sergeant asked me about my musical background and ability. The interview took about a half hour, and I was told a little about the future plans of the entertainment group. Igor and the sergeant decided to give me temporary assignment to the group, which provided musical composition mostly of Russian and Ukrainian material. There were also some German popular selections.

A couple of weeks later, I received a call from Igor. He informed me that he had received permission to work with me in organizing a program for the Ukrainian Guard. Entertainment was scheduled for Sundays only, from seven to nine p.m. The entertainment group treated me fairly and in a businesslike fashion. I was happy because my survival was dependent upon any little accommodation I could make for myself. Igor was especially nice to me, and always managed to prepare some dry foods for me to carry back to the barracks after the entertainment. I always carried my electrician's tool box to these performances, just in case there was an electrical emergency that required my services, and to store food that would be my reserve supply for the next day. The tool box was very handy for a number of reasons. Although I enjoyed working with the entertainment group, there were times when the guards were drunk and would begin shooting at us at random for sport. It was just part of the entertainment. Despite our horror and disbelief, we had to pretend that all was well. When my "friend" Igor was suddenly transferred to an undisclosed location, I was deeply disappointed. My relationship with him was unique. Because of Igor, I carry some of the only good memories of my days at Plaszow.

* * *

One day, as our electricians were working on the electrical poles for the hospital, we noted that a group of people were digging a large pit behind the hospital, supervised by a Ukrainian corporal and about five Ukrainian guards. The general guard of the entire Plaszow camp consisted of 90 percent Ukrainian police and 10 percent German SS (the Ukraine was part of the Soviet Union and, at the time, many Ukrainians defected to the German side during the war). The corporal, speaking to us in German, asked us to help him because the order came that the pit had to be finished by five p.m. We were forced to work to help the others dig the pit for an hour. When we were finished, he thanked us for the beautiful job we did, and then gave us an order to undress and, with the other group from the hospital, go down into the pit. In the meantime, to prove his authority, he shot a number of sick people from the hospital who were not able to walk.

We explained to him that we were electricians, and we pointed to our armbands that we were directed to wear by the commandant. There was somewhat of a commotion at this point; the guards began to hesitate, but we had no choice and went down into the pit. We knew that Amon Goeth had to witness every execution and, while in the pit, we heard the galloping of a horse and knew instinctively that the commandant was coming to supervise the execution. Goeth stopped in front of the pit, called the corporal in charge (who was drunk), and gave him an order to release the group of electricians. We were then escorted by the Ukrainian Guard to our barracks' electrical department. On our way back to the barracks, we could hear the commandant whipping the corporal for giving orders and making decisions without Goeth's knowledge. I was saved form the grave—by the tyrant Goeth. It was the first miracle of many to come. For three days, I was traumatized and could barely function.

I thank G-d I am alive to tell the facts of my survival by coincidence. Another miracle happened when our electrical group, composed of five men and one foreman, including myself, were placing electrical poles for power to the various barracks. We were told that the project had to be finished by six p.m. The engineer and kapo, Mahauf, was in charge of this project. He was granted an additional hour from the Bauleitung (supervisor) as a gesture from the commandant. We were highly suspicious, as the Germans didn't do anything to make it easy for us. With great effort, we finished the project on time. The entire camp had electricity. When we connected the wires from the poles, the engineer hurried to the headquarters of the Bauleitung, informing the commandant that the project was completed on time. As electricians, we had permission to move with relative freedom around the camp, even in the Ukrainian Guard barracks, for electrical work was considered important in the camp. In the vicinity of our work, between ten and fifteen yards away, was a water fountain. After the job was done, I walked over to the water fountain to refresh myself. After splashing water on my face, I was about to take a drink from the fountain when a car suddenly pulled up next to me. I couldn't believe my eyes, for sitting there in his private car was Amon Goeth. His Ukrainian driver, Corporal Janiec, pointed a gun at me, and asked what I was doing there. Since my armband was in plain sight, I told him firmly that I was drinking water. He put his pistol back in the holster, and then told me that because I had told him the truth, he would spare my life. He said that he thought I would answer that I was working there. I was lucky he was in a good mood. Amon Goeth told the driver that the electricians were doing a good job in the camp, and they had developed lots of credibility. I felt so sick after this confrontation that my blood pressure soared for several days. It was considered sabotage to be alone at any time, and I had almost lost my life by simply walking to the fountain to refresh myself. It was a lesson learned.

* * *

Nightfall on December 11, 1942, signified Amon Goeth's birthday celebration at Plaszow camp. He was thirty-four years old. The sun had just set and the sound of cars could be heard as the guests arrived at the commandant's mansion up on the hill. In the camp down below sounds of Johann Strauss' waltzes echoed through the night air.

Tomasz Kulinsky (his given name was Henryk Schreiber; as was common with Jews he changed his Jewish-sounding name) and I had been standing outside our military-style barracks in Section B-West, just staring at the top of the hill. We were a few hundred feet away from the festivities, but we might as well have been on another planet.

At five a.m. we were awakened from a fitful sleep when the loudspeakers suddenly blared with orders for all inmates in Section B-West to report for a special roll call by 5:30 a.m. at the Appelplatz (camp square); latecomers would be shot. The Appelplatz was where Jews assembled each morning for roll call and where Jews were beaten, shot, hanged, or made to suffer all sorts of indignities. The announcement to assemble at the square was usually accompanied by Amon Goeth's voice over the loudspeaker—"Everyone who is alive is to come to the Appelplatz." The inmates suffered unimaginable terror at the hands of Amon Goeth; we were a barracks town of 20,000 unquiet Jews. This was part of the camp's reality—from time to time a quota had to be shipped to a death camp. This was one of those occasions, and it involved Section B-West.

At 5:20 a.m. all inmates from Section B-West were on their way to the square, with the exception of eleven of us from Barracks #7 (my barracks). I discussed the issue with those remaining and came to this conclusion: "I am not going, and that is that. Is anyone staying with me?" I knew that we were risking our lives, but I had decided to take a stand. To the others I am sure that my voice reflected a sense of determination, my face frozen into a mask of defiance. Without further comment, I walked back toward the barracks with the intention of hiding underneath (a hiding place where I would also sing and conduct services with the other inmates). Ten other inmates silently followed.

The head count at the square was completed at 6:05 a.m. It was at this point that the SS officers in charge realized that eleven inmates were missing. "No one moves until we find these criminals. They will be shot," roared the SS assistant under camp commandant, Sturmfuhrer Schultz. Specially trained dogs, notorious for finding escapees, were called in and the manhunt began in earnest. The dogs led their SS masters, with vicious barking echoing throughout the camp. We realized that our discovery was imminent. The sounds of impending calamity, and loss of our cover, reached a feverish pitch as the dogs moved in on us. We knew that momentarily it would all be over.

The anticipated disaster did not happen. As if by a miracle, the barking began to fade into the distance. The dogs had changed direction. About twenty minutes later, at 7:12 a.m., the official whistle sounded, indicating that the search had ended. As it turned out, a German cantina (food storage area) nearby distracted the attention of the dogs. It seemed that the dogs preferred the smell of salami to that of human flesh…or could it be that the dogs had a higher level of integrity than their German master?

Several hundred of the weak and infirm inmates were shipped to their deaths at Treblinka as a result of that particular roll call. Approximately 6,000 inmates remained and were returned to their barracks. It was heartbreaking for us to see our fellow inmates sent to their untimely deaths, but there was simply nothing we could do to stop the madness.

Those of us in hiding came out and mingled with those who had been spared. The Germans were not able to tell which of us had been missing earlier, much to our relief. Another remarkable day had ended at Plaszow camp. I truly believe that my survival was destined. Each time I faced another day of terror, I looked up to the heavens and prayed to my mother and father. Only then did I know that I would survive this horror of horrors.

* * *

The camp at Plaszow was initially a labor camp for Jews (Arbeitslager). The name was changed to a forced labor camp (Zwansarbeitslager) after imprisonment of some Poles and citizens from other countries. It was at this point that Amon Goeth became the official commandant of Plaszow camp. The building of a larger camp began at the end of October 1942. People who worked in the camp and lived outside the camp boundaries had to remain inside to work on construction. At this time I was locked in as a prisoner. We all worked feverishly, under the command of the Nazis, along with the Jews brought in every day from the ghetto. The camp was divided into three parts: the women's barracks section situated on the top of the hill; the men's section in the outer perimeter of the camp; and the Polish inmates in the middle of the camp. In August 1944 the Germans conducted a terror *Aktion* in the streets of Cracow. They captured 7,000 civilian Polish men (non-Jews) and brought them to the Polish sector of Plaszow for three to six months. They were forced to do hard labor but were fed better than the Jews and were not massacred.

When Amon Goeth became the camp leader, he submitted a proposal to the Nazi authorities for a crematorium to be built at the new Cracow-Plaszow camp. His plan was rejected, as the High Command felt that the camp would have to be liquidated as the Russian offensive moved farther and farther to the west. The Gestapo was antagonistic toward Goeth and his luxurious lifestyle. They conducted periodic investigations into Goeth's activities, with high-ranking visitors coming to Plaszow to see how the camp was run and if there were abuses, as they suspected. Goeth did not want to be returned to Germany, where food was scarce and his standard of living would dramatically change. So he found little ways to keep his abuses from the authorities.

Plaszow Designated as Concentration Camp

It was not until the early months of 1944 that Plaszow was officially recognized as a concentration camp (Konzentrazionlager), a branch of Maidanek Concentration Camp. After Auschwitz, Plaszow was the second largest camp in the Cracow district (Auschwitz had 405,000 prisoners, half of them Jews, the rest non-Jewish Poles. These prisoners were registered and tattooed with a prisoner number on the left arm. Ironically, Auschwitz land was owned by Jews).

After Plaszow became a concentration camp, inmates found it safer to encounter Amon Goeth. He was no longer permitted to shoot prisoners on the spot. They could now be destroyed only by due process—there had to be a hearing, and records sent in triplicate to the chiefs in Oranienburg. Later, Goeth did find ways to circumvent the rules. The prisoners knew that when Goeth wore his Tyrolean "hunting" hat, killings or beatings would soon take place. It was not unusual for a worker to be killed on the spot for no reason and no warning given. The remaining slave laborers would become fearful, thus producing even more intensive work.

The Plaszow camp was built on a hilly, rocky spot and stretched beyond the hills to an area full of malaria-ridden swamps. The hills had to be planed down and the swamps drained—all by Jewish hands and Jewish blood. Double rows of barbed wires surrounded the camp, with high poles of concrete to support the barbed wire. The barbed wire was then charged with high voltage electricity, enough to cause instant death. Also, six strategically placed watchtowers, with German and Ukrainian guards posted around the clock with machine guns and powerful semiautomatic machine pistols as back up, reinforced the camp's security.

Beyond the barbed wire, up on a hill, were mass graves. This hill also served as an execution site for Jews selected for hard labor. Those selected for execution had to undress themselves. They were examined for gold teeth and other workers were ordered to remove the teeth for Nazi use, before or after they were executed. The bodies were then thrown into the pit that was dug for that purpose, more than likely by the victims themselves.

The industrial building operations at Plaszow were housed in rows of barracks, each with a specialized industry—sewing, carpentry, shoe-making, paper product manufacturing, locksmithing, printing, and glass products, to name a few. The Kabel Company (where I had been employed outside the camp) had 300 prison employees in Plaszow camp. There were also stores that had been moved from Cracow Ghetto to the camp.

There were an infirmary and a hospital with Jewish doctors taking care of sick inmates. The German and Ukrainian soldiers and guards had separate hospital facilities.

The electrical department at Plaszow was divided into three groups: day and night shifts, and a special emergency-call group. The night shift faced the danger and the unpredictable, especially when providing electrical service to the camp towers. Each tower had a number and was manned with two Ukrainian guards, one machine gun, reflectors, and a telephone connected to the headquarters' office of the superior commandant in charge. Our equipment consisted of our "special" electrical group armbands, a flashlight, and a tool box. In the beginning, it became a tradition for the Ukrainians to look for opportunities to take away everything and anything of value from us (they knew there was much smuggling of food and money into Plaszow). They did this for fun and enjoyment. We were at their mercy.

The Ukrainian guards wore black uniforms and were used by the Nazis to implement orders issued by the German High Command authorities. Most of these orders took the form of punishment, which was a daily occurrence. Beatings were twenty-five, fifty, or one hundred lashes. The prisoners were made to count each lash. If they missed, the lashing would start all over again. The Ukrainians were well suited to the job, as it fit perfectly into the centuries old pattern of savage hatred and sadistic treatment of the Jews.

The Ukrainian guards changed shifts in groups of fifteen to thirty guards. The group would march, singing Russian marching songs as they approached their stations. We were awed by the performance, all of this in spite of the chaos and hardship around us.

* * *

With the liquidation of the Cracow Ghetto, and all the other surrounding camps, there were now 25,000 Jews imprisoned in the Plaszow camp (of those remaining in the Cracow Ghetto 8,000 were sent to Plaszow, 2,000 killed on the spot, and 4,000 were sent to Auschwitz and other extermination camps for immediate execution). I was already at Plaszow and did not personally witness the event. There was a reign of terror throughout the ghetto: doctors, nurses, and hospital patients were killed. SS soldiers broke into apartments, grabbed suitcases with belongings, and tossed them into the streets. People were beaten and shot during the terrible siege and then loaded into boxcars like cattle. Many died of suffocation. This final liquidation of the Cracow Ghetto was carried out by the will of SS Officer Willi Haase. A little more than one year later, April 1944, Amon Goeth was ordered to exhume and incinerate the bodies of more than 10,000 Jews killed at Plaszow and the Cracow Ghetto massacre.

* * *

For a while, things were relatively quiet; no shooting, no terror, and even the food rations improved. We all knew instinctively that we could expect some dramatic events after every period of calm. This was not pure speculation. We were nervous for good reason, for one spring day a new group of about thirty young male and female SS of various ranks arrived and paraded in the camp. No doubt they had come to gain experience and improve their managerial skills. It was a stepping-stone to further promotions. After a few days, the entire group was given authority to force inmates to work at a faster pace. They were particularly harsh on the Polish Gentile inmates, most of whom were part of the Polish underground who brought us news of the outside world and the hope that we would one day be free.

Although there were no shootings, the SS men and women displayed their sadistic natures by crippling, beating and torturing, and demoralizing the inmates. I happened to be in the wrong place at the wrong time while repairing one of the electric wires in the Polish inmates' living quarters. I was savagely beaten, almost into unconsciousness. My head and right hand were bleeding profusely. The kapo, a front-runner who was responsible for the entire electrical group, sent me to the emergency field hospital for treatment. A couple of months later, I developed a phlegmona (swelling) in my right hand, with high fever. The doctor examined my hand and told me I needed surgery immediately. I knew very well that if I didn't recover in thirty days, I was in extreme danger of extermination; no questions asked. Fortunately one day before "cleaning house" I was discharged. Ridding the camp of people too sick to work was routine procedure and I thanked G-d that I was again spared. The medical authority of the hospital, Dr. Weiss, saved my life.

The medicine smuggled into the camp by my aunt Regina Hendel was also a saving grace, since the Plaszow hospital was ill equipped for medical emergencies. Of course I always recite a prayer of Thanksgiving when a major miracle saves my life. My scars, which remain a perpetual reminder of the experience, healed almost completely within four weeks of treatment. I have always believed in G-d's wonders, and also believe that I am alive today for the purpose of passing along my story, and those of others, to the next generation.

* * *

About four weeks after my recovery, my uncle Simon, aunt Regina, and cousin Samy Grunwald, were delivered to the Plaszow camp, as Jews with false Hungarian citizenship papers. Word spread quickly of newcomers arriving at the camp—we were all looking for family members who had somehow survived. As soon as a name was known, sometimes with the help of inmates working in the registration and admitting office of the camp, we would pass it on to other inmates throughout the day until a connection was made with a family member. We had an extraordinary grapevine for passing on and gathering information. Sadly, we witnessed the execution of my uncle and cousin in the square. My aunt Regina was more fortunate. She was transferred to Bergen-Belsen. I thank G-d for sparing my dear aunt's life. Perhaps the fact that she was a very creative person helped to spare her life. After the liberation of Bergen-Belsen in 1945, aunt Regina Grunwald emigrated to Brazil, where she passed away some years ago. I never saw her after Plaszow but thought of her for many years.

At this period of time, Oskar Schindler would routinely visit Plaszow to meet with Commandant Amon Goeth. The inmates recognized Schindler's truck as it moved in and out of the camp with the name of his factory, DEF (Deutsch Emailwaren Fabrik), prominently displayed on the side of his truck. We had heard that Schindler gained Goeth's cooperation in giving him workers for his factory in return for his "gratitude." Payoffs were made to the German regime in the form of material goods and cash, much of it for Amon Goeth himself. Oskar Schindler deceived Goeth into believing he was his good friend, in order to obtain workers for his factory. Oskar actually despised Goeth. Interestingly, they shared similar backgrounds: born the same year, raised Catholic, a weakness for liquor and women, and a massive physique. Goeth wanted Oskar to move his plant into Plaszow camp. Instead, Oskar built a sub camp at Plaszow in his own factory yard in order to keep prisoners away from the horror of Plaszow. The requirements for an SS forced labor sub camp included nine foot tall fences, watchtowers at given intervals around the camp, latrines, barracks, a clinic, dental office, bathhouse and delousing complex, a barbershop, food store, laundry, barracks office, and a guard block. Herr Direktor Schindler incurred the cost for all of it.

At first, Schindler was seen as a war profiteer, interested only in amassing personal wealth. Later, we learned that he was a "Righteous Person" who saved some 1,200 Jews who worked his factory on the incorrect assumption by the Germans that they were vital workers producing ammunition for the Germans. Initially, Schindler was manufacturing enamel cookware for the German occupation administration but later converted to armaments production when the Soviet army approached Cracow. The Jewish workers never produced a single artillery shell that passed quality control of the Germans. Oskar recalibrated all his equipment to give false readings to the German inspectors who came through the plant. His factory was a front for protecting the Jews. He spent millions of his own personal fortune to provide a safe haven for his people.

At the time he reestablished his firm from cookware to munitions, Schindler moved to a new location in Brunnlitz, Czechoslovakia. During the transfer his workers were inadvertently shipped to Gross-Rosen camp (800 of the Jewish men) and to Birkenau (300 of the Jewish women). Schindler was able to arrange for their safe return to his factory where he provided them with food, medical care, shelter, and a safe place where they were allowed to practice their religion. He also launched a rescue operation to take 100 stranded and nearly frozen Jews from Goleszow camp in a rail car to his factory where they were nourished back to health. Schindler told all his workers that they would be safe and live through the war. He kept his promise (in 1962, Oskar Schindler was impoverished, but endured in the knowledge of those Jews whom he had saved; he was helped financially for the remainder of his life by "Schindler Jews").

* * *

On the morning of September 30, 1943, at 10:15 a.m., Corporal Janiec Radinow, of the Ukrainian camp Police Auxiliary, approached Work Unit 6X where I was working. He shouted, "To the square for cleaning duty. Guests are coming and it has to be spotlessly clean." Keeping things clean was a major idiosyncrasy of the Germans. The latrines were heavily doused with pine disinfectant to prevent the spread of disease, one of their greatest fears. When the work unit of thirty inmates, including myself, reached the square, brooms were waiting and the work started immediately. To remind the inmates of their "supervisory" authority, the Ukrainian guards, with Corporal Janiec in charge, used their leather whips unsparingly on the helpless inmates. By 11:15 a.m., Janiec gave an indication that the square was ready for visitors.

The inmates placed the brooms on a waiting truck and then remained standing in the center of the square. The guests were SS officers from other prison camps. The commandant was deeply involved in briefing his visitors about camp procedures. Questions were frequently asked. An observer would have gotten the impression that this was all part of a high-level business seminar. At a specific moment, the commandant turned to his assistant Sturmfuhrer, Franz Bohm, and told him to proceed immediately. The thirty inmates were ordered to stand in formations of five with ten feet between each row.

Amon Goeth was wearing his Tyrolean hunting hat, so the inmates knew that today there would be lots of bloodshed. Showtime was about to begin, in the form of Goeth's favorite sport—hunting. "When I whistle," shouted Goeth, "you animals start running." There was no choice but to obey the order. The whistle was heard and the horrified inmates started to run for their lives. Commandant Goeth was shooting his gun in the air and then aimed at the running inmates. The first three shots hit three inmates. One fell right next to me. Applause was heard. The guests were impressed with Goeth's marksmanship. More shots were heard and more inmates were falling, some in silence, others with agonizing groans. Bullets filled the air. It was a war zone. "When will my turn come?" was the only thought that passed through my mind. Only a few inmates were still running, as was I. I realized that the far end of the square was near. The shots stopped, and Goeth's voice was heard, "This is the end of the exercise. Stop where you are."

Accompanied by his "distinguished" guests, Goeth marched along the square. He looked at the survivors and remarked, "I used exactly thirty bullets, and that means only four shots were missed." That is a wonderful record," said one of the guests. "You are a real marksman," said another. Goeth's assistant, Bohm, walked behind the group, examining the victims on the ground. He put his pistol to the heads of those who still appeared to be alive and shot them. "This is our Humanitarian Policy," explained Goeth. He then added, "Gentlemen, it seems to be time for lunch. Chef Springer has prepared a fine meal for us, with Schnitzel ala Holstein, potato salad, cabbage salad, fine Westphalian wine, and Kirschen torte for dessert." The guests seemed to like the idea, since it was time for a pleasant break after a long and tiresome morning of briefings.

Corporal Schultz approached the remaining four who had survived and told us to join Work Unit 31. "Your lunch is waiting there," he added, laughing. As we walked to Unit 31, I saw from a distance that Unit F-7 was busily loading the dead bodies in the square onto carts for disposal. As it turned out, our lunch was the usual potato peels in hot water—they called this soup (since food was being smuggled in, I was well fed and weighing about 120 pounds). In the summer of 1944, the Jewish Joint Distribution Committee of America began sending food products for prisoners. Most of the food fell into German hands, but our soups were perceptibly thicker and tastier than before. I recall that one month the inmates had tapioca every night for dinner. This was our entire meal; nevertheless, it was a welcome change of diet for us. I think the International Red Cross may have supplied the tapioca.

In another incident that I call the "tombstone performance," Goeth brought officers in training to a site where I had been assigned to help build the Plaszow road (made from Jewish tombstones). We worked in groups of four, two men on each end of a stretcher-like contraption piled high with tombstones. To impress his guests, Goeth suddenly gave the command, "Go faster" ("mach schnell"). We had no choice but to run with the tombstones as Goeth started shooting at us to entertain his guests. Miraculously, I lived to tell the story of another unspeakable incident of terror and humiliation.

* * *

One night, in the fall of 1944, at about two a.m., I happened to be on emergency call (we worked in teams of two men for all calls) with my cousin, Zyga Riegelhaupt. Zyga was a full electrical mechanic with four to five people under his charge. No one knew we were related, other than the inmates. He and I would talk about whether or not we would survive. It was a good feeling to know I had some family near me. This particular night we received an order to report to Tower #4, in total darkness. We came up to the tower and were amazed to see the machine gun dismantled, with the wires cut off from the main line. We found a note left by the Ukrainian guards containing the following words: "The war is almost over and we are joining the partisans. You will be liberated soon." We left the tower with such a sweet feeling of satisfaction, despite our hunger and exhaustion. After this incident, the group manning the towers changed to one German and one Ukrainian.

In August 1944 we knew the Russians were advancing, pushing the German army farther and farther west. The Germans activated their plans for demobilization of the Plaszow camp on August 6. Prisoners received an order that everyone was to be ready to depart Plaszow. On September 13, 1944, the SS arrested Amon Goeth. It was not until October 1944 that actual demobilization of the camp took place (throughout the war, the Nazis were worried the Soviets would find evidence of the hundreds of thousands of victims who had been killed, and evacuating prisoners was part of their plan to avoid detection).[9]

Transfer to Gross-Rosen

Gross-Rosen was a primarily German transit camp for the people assigned to forced labor in different parts of Germany and Austria. Some inmates remained at Gross-Rosen to dig canals, build roads, and work on river control projects. There was also gassing of inmates at Gross-Rosen. The camp was composed of many nationalities. For the first time we came across German born inmates who had been the head kapos, supervising administrative offices, registrations, food distributions, and special "clothing" (camp uniforms). They were well dressed, clean, and healthy and wore normal suits and shoes, rather than camp uniforms. The only way you could recognize them as German inmates was by their special armbands, marked with the Haftling (inmate's number).

When we arrived at the camp square, we were "received" by a group of professional boxers (and prisoners), all wearing boxing gloves. They were sparring with the newcomer prison inmates, while the camp orchestra played a happy, loud number that covered the sounds of the boxing match and the terrified inmates (music was often used during

---

[9] By October 1944, Germany was losing the war, as the Soviets were gaining ground daily. It was time to cover up the evidence of the "final solution" so the world would never know. Using prisoners as laborers, they dismantled the gas chambers at Auschwitz-Birkenau (which were some two miles apart and connected by rail). The following month, they began to demolish the crematoria and send the usable parts back to Germany.

times when children were taken away from their mothers, and families were being separated for extermination; the music muffled the sounds of people screaming for mercy). After this boxing "game," we were lined up for registration. It was late and we were cold and hungry. One half of our total transport was sent to the field hospital; the other, including myself, were sent to the "showers," which we knew could be a matter of life or death. The shower for the living was a real shower with running water; the shower for the dead was a gas chamber masquerading as a shower. The gas chambers were used to exterminate Jews when they were no longer useful.

As we waited undressed in the bitter cold for hours, we were lined up alphabetically. Because my name began with "H" I was in the middle of the line. I could tell from where I stood, close to the entrance of the shower building, that it was the shower for the living (and not a gas chamber, as we feared). We were told that we would be in quarantine for a couple of weeks. We were deloused by having our heads shaved. In some camps, head shaving or leaving a stripe of hair down the center was used to identify prisoners. Prisoners' hair was of economic value to German companies that used it in mattress stuffing, coat linings, slippers, hair-yarn socks for U-boat crews and other footwear.

We were now under the authority of the building administration affiliated with the NSDAP (the Nazi party's national socialist regime). The first sign of improvement in our treatment was the food and medical treatment. We began to breathe a kind of "fresh air." The treatment during this quarantine period was such that we received a bowl of milk every day (with oatmeal), were served lunch, and also meat with potatoes for the evening meals, all ordered by the NSDAP authority. We were given new clothing and shoes. In other words, a complete overhaul. It seemed we had suddenly become a precious commodity. The pressure and fear subsided a little, as we felt a certain measure of protection by this extraordinary change. It offered hope in the midst of outrageous abuse.

Evacuation to Ludwigsdorf

Gross-Rosen began to evacuate inmates to other forced labor camps in Germany. Because of my identity as an electrician, I was assigned to a small town in Ludwigsdorf, Germany. To our surprise, it looked like first-class accommodations. It was a facility with new barracks, fresh linens and blankets, a new kitchen, but unfortunately little food. We suffered from severe hunger, and the Germans didn't have food either. Each week the sick people, and those who needed dental work, were picked up and taken to a nearby hospital for treatment. The terror and fear disappeared completely. The guard was composed of about fifty retired Wehrmacht soldiers and the camp commandant was an SS Obersharfuhrer (sergeant).

By November 1944 I was engaged in helping to build a tunnel for the Luftwaffe. The tunnels served as an underground hiding place for secret military equipment. Five connected tunnels were built. Our group consisted of four German electrical specialists and five inmates who reported to the group leader. We were assigned to work in the tunnels, and sometimes on the electrical poles. The winter was torture, constant below zero temperature. We had to fight cold and hunger under the most hazardous conditions. After many months of slave labor in the tunnels at Ludwigsdorf, I was transferred to Ebensee.

Ebensee Concentration Camp

In mid-December 1944, an order came from Bauleitung headquarters that the camp be evacuated to Mauthausen, Austria. The situation had now reversed itself completely. Our group marched day and night until we reached a railway station with open boxcars. (I can still remember the shoes I wore with wooden soles, not too desirable for walking day and night.) The moon was our light in the darkness. Once in the open boxcars, there was no food or water. The wind was bitterly cold.

About one third of the 2,500 prisoners survived this ordeal. Finally, after several days of torture, a truck came from the Wehrmacht and distributed cans of first-class meat and hot, ersatz coffee. Was this good fortune, or a political move against the SS policy? We wondered.

When we reached the Mauthausen station, we were told that there was no room for us at Ebensee Concentration Camp. It was one of more than forty sub camps of the concentration camp at Mauthausen. We were placed in a barn with stables, until our group could be absorbed into the camp. We ate potatoes and grass. The allied forces had been surrounding the area. We watched as the German army retreated. The panic and chaos shown by the Germans indicated to us that the war was coming to an end.

* * *

In early January 1945, we reached Ebensee camp in upper Austria where we stayed until the liberation on May 6, 1945. When we saw the condition of the inmates held there, like living skeletons, we were gripped with sadness and anger. The inhumane treatment suffered by the Ebensee prisoners at the hands of their captors was beyond belief. The air was heavy around us with smog and the smell of human flesh. We learned from other prisoners in the camp that Ebensee was composed of different nationalities, including Russian, Italian, German, French, Greek, Polish, Hungarian, and Yugoslavian inmates, with Jews in the minority. We were told that 27,000 prisoners were brought into the camp; more than 8,200 of them died before liberation. Prisoners were made to drive gigantic subterranean tunnels into the mountain. Relocated into these tunnels, the Peenemunde rocket research center was protected from air raids.

Such were the catastrophic conditions that we faced at Ebensee, conditions so deplorable as to defy description. We frantically ate everything we could chew from the ground: leaves, grass, and insects. Some ate coal and died from it. The average weight of the prisoners was sixty to eighty pounds. On the day of liberation, I weighed about ninety-five pounds. I was one of the lucky ones. I survived by my instincts.

We remained at Ebensee in poor health, in unbelievably unsanitary conditions, and with no food or water (other than the freshly fallen snow). Hunger, fear, and cold were our constant companions. The German army was hungry, too, and they were running. The winter and the hunger killed hundreds, and sometimes thousands, every day.

The Ebensee Concentration Camp was equipped with two large crematoria that burned day and night. Obersturmfuhrer (SS Officer) Anton Ganz was the commandant of Ebensee. We heard through the underground that the liquidation of the entire population of the camp had been ordered. At this time, we had 18,000 inmates in the camp, all-working in the tunnels. In anticipation of the arrival of the Allied Forces, the tunnels had been mined and were ready to be used to annihilate the inmates, to leave no trace of the inhumanity we had endured. We heard allied, artillery bombardment throughout the night, moving in our direction. The Americans were a few kilometers away. The SS guard had left two days before and were replaced by older, retired personnel. This really wasn't necessary, as the entire camp was like one huge hospital. Most of the inmates couldn't walk (I had the strength to walk short distances), and we were all sick and numb from the devastation. Ebensee was designed to hold five to six thousand people. It housed 27,000. Survivors recall Ebensee as one of the worst camps of all. The only reason for the camp's existence was to provide manpower for the tunnels. The advantage of the concentration camp in Ebensee was that in 1944 it was relatively small, so prisoners could get to know one another. The numerous work details outside the camp, and the contacts with the civilian workers, favored the smuggling of food items and documents and allowed information to get into the camp. The disadvantage was that the SS could control the prisoners more easily.

As described (by liberated prisoners) before the American Investigative Committee, "There was an absolute lack of clothing, shoes, and food. Ninety percent of the prisoners had no overcoats, sweaters, or gloves to wear in their work details, and many of them were barefooted, without socks or shoes. They wrapped their feet in a piece of paper, a rag, or a piece of blanket. This, of course, was considered sabotage and was punished with twenty-five lashes on one's back. . ." It was common for prisoners to die while on work details. They died on the camp streets, and the hospital was so overloaded that four to five patients had to lie in a single bunk.

* * *

It was one of those freezing, grey mornings. Everything around us was icy and bleak. During morning roll call, (the start of another day of torture and twelve-hours of forced labor in the tunnels) I met my friend, Josele Firebaum, at the northeast corner of Barracks #7. I told him that as long as we were alive there was hope. Josele and I met at Ebensee. He was about seventeen years old (I was then twenty two), of orthodox background, and he also had lost his family. Josele was always praying and wanted to be smuggled by the underground who were bringing survivors to Israel. We realized that we had to safeguard what was Jewish. . .the essence of our existence. Josele and I made it our daily practice to meet and say a short prayer and then recite a Jewish poem, or sing a Jewish song softly. This was the most we were able to do within the few minutes we had together. On that particular day, we sang an old, short Jewish folk song we both knew, "A Brevele Der Mame" (a letter to Mother). Those few minutes Joesle and I had together, while tears were freezing our cheeks, was the only spark of light in the horror of what we had faced. I wanted so much to share all of the experience with Josele, but he did not live to see the liberation. One morning he did not show up for our morning get-together, and I never saw him again.

CRACOW - POLAND - 1933

Hauben family wedding photo. Far left back row is William Hauben, brother Romek standing to his left. Front row is William's mother, Gertrude, third from left, Aunt Regina Hendel is seated to Gertrude's left.
c 1932 Cracow, Poland

Family photograph of twelve Hauben brothers and sisters. Far left in front is William's parents. Grandparents are shown in front row to left and right of center. c 1931. Cracow, Poland.

William's grandfather, Fievel, and other family in-laws at Cracow wedding. c 1935

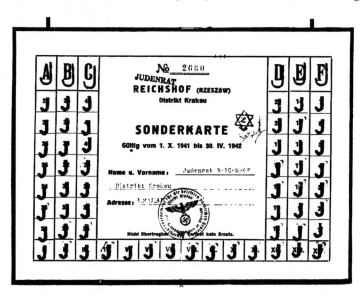

Judenrat ID Card required for all Jews in the district of Cracow during German occupation. c 1941

פ נ

רחל הויבען

בת ר ישראל זל

יג כה אייר תרפט

שרגא פייבל הויבען

בן ר זאב יגה הכהן זל

יג ב מרחשון תרחץ

KU CZCI ZAMORDOWANYCH W OBOZACH KONCEN

PRZEZ ZBIROW NIEMIECKICH W LATACH 1942-4

SYNOWIE: **ZYGMUNT** Z ZONA I SYNEM

LAZAR Z ZONA I 2MA CORKAMI

SZYMON Z ZONA I 2MA CORKAMI

MARKUS Z ZONA I CORECZKA

SIMON

CORKI **SALOMEA** Z MEZEM CORRA I SYNEM

FRANCISZKA Z SYNEM

PAULINA Z MEZEM I CORECZKA

ROZA Z MEZEM I SYNKIEM

ZIEC **EMANUEL FIGATNER** Z SYNAMI

This headstone was erected in honor of William's grandfather Fievel & grand-
mother Rachel Hauben, a number of years before World War II. During the war, in
the years 1942-1945, most Hauben family members were lost in the Holocaust. As a
tribute and living memorial for future generations, the names of ten lost Hauben
family members and their children were added to the original headstone, in blessed
memory. Cracow, Poland

R.° CONSERVATORIO DI MUSICA "GIUSEPPE VERDI„

TORINO

Si certifica che ..i.l. Signor *Hauben Guglielmo*

nato a *Cracovia* da *fu Salomone* e da ....

è inscritto in questo Conservatorio, per l'anno scolastico corrente

(19 *46* / 19 *47*) quale allievo del *3°* anno della Scuola di

Canto e Materie complementari

Rilasciato a richiesta dell'interessato per essere presentato all'

Unrra Italian Mission

Camp Operations Division

Torino (It. 17) Campo (Grugliasco)

Torino, li *24 Ottobre* 194*6*

Giuseppe Verdi Conservatory of Music certificate of admissions.
October 24, 1946

© Neil Folberg, "Interior, Stara Synagogue," Cracow, Poland from And I shall
Dwell Among Them: Historic synagogues of the world, Aperture, New York,
1995. The Alte Shul is a Gothic structure built in the fourteenth century. During
World War II, the Nazis desecrated and looted the synagogue, and murdered
thousands of Jews there. They used the synagogue for storage and as a stable for
horses before ultimately destroying it. The Alte Shul was rebuilt in the late 1950's
and currently houses the Judaica Branch of the Historical Museum of Krakow,
with a collection of Judaica from the 17th, 18th, and 20th centuries.

Aunt Regina Hendel. Tel Aviv, Israel. c 1960

William is shown at left of photo, while employed by the Jewish Brigade in Milan, Italy. 1946

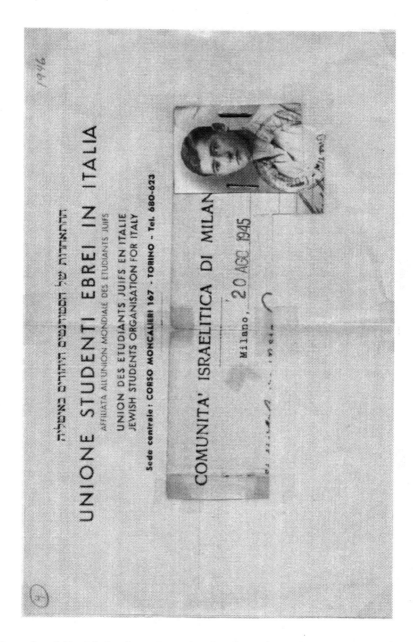

Letterhead: Jewish Students Organization for Italy, and Jewish community of Milan. 1945.

Starved prisoners, nearly dead from hunger, pose in Ebensee camp in the Austrian Alps, on May 15, 1945, nine days after Liberation Day. William Hauben is in the back row center looking over the heads of his fellow prisoners. Courtesy of the National Archives, U.S. Signal Corps photo by Lt. A.E. Samuelson.

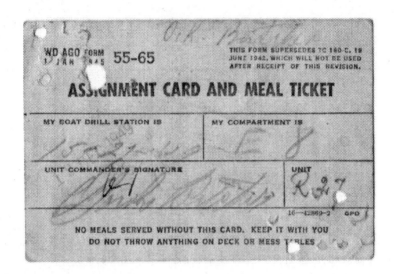

Assignment card and meal ticket for trip by boat to the U.S. December 1949.

British Embassy registration card No. M465. March 1946.

ID card for civilian internees of Mauthausen. 1945.

Odpis   wierzytelny .

Kraków, dnia 30 sierpnia 1948. <u>Zaświadczenie.</u> Jako sekretarz
i założyciel powszechnej " CHEDER IWRI " i gimnazjum " TACHKE-
MONI " w Krakowie,zaświadczam, że Wilhelm H A U B E N ur.
dnia 26.III.1922 r.syn Salomona i Gustawy z Grünwaldów uczęsz-
czał w latach 1929 - 1937 do, wyżej wspomnianych szkól. - Wolf
Bauminger mp. Wolf Bauminger. - Autentyczność podpisu ob.Wolfa
Baumingera - obecnie sekretarza niżej podpisanego Stowarzy s e-
nia - potwierdzamy. Za Zarząd : Stowarzyszenie " Mizrachi Tora
Waawoda " w Krakowie, ul. Miodowa 26. - Drezner mp.Auerbach mp.
Zarząd Żyd.Kongregacji Wyznaniowej w Krakowie zaświadcza autentyczność podpisu ob. Wolfa Baumingera, sekretarza Stow." Miz-
rachi Tora Waawoda.Kraków, dnia 1 września 1948 r. Za Zarząd:
Sternberg mp. L.S. -

    Nr.Rep. 5838/1948.-
    Stwierdzam zgodność tego odpisu z okazanym
    mi oryginałem.
    Pobrano od tego odpisu opłatę skarbową po myśli
    tabeli opłat skarbowych poz.2. lit.e. w kwocie
    10 zł. i należytość notarialną z § 21.tar.not. 60 zł.
    i z § 26 tejże tar.50 zł.

        W Krakowie,dnia dwudziestego ósmego września
        tysiąc dziewięćset czterdziestego ósmego roku.

Affirmation of William Hauben's identification for the Olivetti Company. 1948

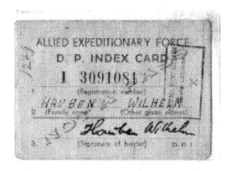

Allied Expeditionary Forces ID card
for displaced persons, No. 13091081.
August 1945.

Filing petition for naturalization
in the U.S. District Court,
Chicago, Illinois. 1955

ISSUED TO THE HOLDER

A. Camp Entry Kit: *Date* ....By .... **B. Clothing on Admittance:** *Date* .... *By* ....

including .... *Blankets* ....

17/1/49 - 4 Blankets 1 armycot

C. Replacement Items:	Date	By	Date	By	Date	By	Date	By	Date	By
Hat/Cap	12/1/49	M								
Overcoat	1									
Jacket/Sweater	11									
Shirt/Blouse	1		16/1/49	1	23-4-49	1				
Trousers/Shorts	4									
Skirt/Slacks			4/49	4	" " "	3				
Dress/Slip (Wool/cotton) Suit Pour .					" " "	1				
Under Shirt/Under pants			1 4/49	1	" " "	1-1				
Pairs of Stockings.	2				" " "	1				
Sleeping Garment . Towel . .					" " "	1				
Shoes	1				" " "	1R				

D. Equipment Returned:

Camp .... *Date* ...... *Yes* ...... *No.* .... *Initials* ......

PAGE 5   PAGE 6

Control Book for displaced persons and refugees. 1946

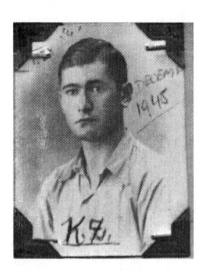

*William Hauben, five months after liberation at Ebensee camp. December 1945.
He was a displaced person until the Jewish Brigade arranged for evacuation to
Modena, Italy.*

U.S.DESK
I.R.O.PROCESSING CENTER
BAGNOLI

ROUTING PROCESSING SHEET

E.C.No. 94308

NAME: *Hansen Wilhelm*

SPONSOR *Usma*

No.Persons on Assurance: 1

1. This sheet will be retained by Displaced Person until completion of processing
2. Consult frequently routing lists on Camp Bulltin Board.

PROCESSING STAGES	LOCATION	TIME	CHECKED BY	DATE
1. F. F. I.	Bl.P.Room 40		Date 21.10.49	
2. Registration-Billeting				
a) Reception	Bl.P Room 32	13, 00. h		21-10-49
b) Movement	Bl.Q Room 6-7	14 45		21 X 49
3. I.R.O. US Desk				
a) Information-Registration	Bl.Q Room 41	15, 20		21.10.49
b) Checking of documents	Bl.Q Room 30			
c) Resettlement Registration Interview	Bl.Q Room 43			
d) Fingerprinting	Bl.Q Room 44			
e)				
4. Voluntary Agencies				
a) C.W.S.	Bl.Q Room 14			
b) HIAS - A.J.D.C.	Bl.Q Room 20	14 55	Neuefeld	21.10.45
c) N.C.W.C.	Bl.Q Room 22			
5. I.R.O. Medical Section				
a) R & R Medical Registration	P Room 30	11.30		
b) X Ray		28.10.49		28-X-19
c) Blood Test				
d) Physical Examination				
e)				
6. U.S. DP Commission				
a) Interview	Bl.Q Room 38	1500		25.10.49
b)				
7. U.S.PUBLIC HEALTH SERVICE	Bl.P Room 6			
8. U.S.CONSULAR SERVICE	Bl.Q Room 15		Perrone	NOV 4 1949
9. I.R.O. US Desk				22-11-49
a) Registration f.Embarkation	Q Room 45			
b) Outregistration	Bl.QRoom 41			
10.Registration-Billeting (for Outregistration)	Bl. Q Room 6-7			
11. U.S.Immigration				
12.International Movements Office				

Route-processing sheet for displaced persons. Bagnoli, Italy. 1949.

AMERICAN JOINT DISTRIBUTION COMMITTEE

Emigration Office - Milan

Milan ...July 23rd, 49......
Via Sangallo 40 - Tel. 293.493

Our letter No. ....7784........
European Case No. ..94308......

Mr. Hauben Wilhelm
Studentshostel
T u r i n

        Reference is made to your application for Emigration
to the United States of America under the terms of the DP bill.

This Office is glad to inform you that our Rome HQ is holding
on your behalf (XHXXXIXKM - community) job and housing assurance in the profession of mechanic.......... in ..Chicago....

You are requested to submit to us following documentation:

    a) Original birth certificate and photocopie
    b) Original marriage certificate and photocopie
    c) Good conduct certificate in duplicate.
    d) 3 photos per capita
    e) a document showing your entry into Italy, Austria,
       Germany (DP Countries) before December 22nd, 45.

Kindly acknowledge receipt of this letter by return of mail.
Please note that also two photocopies of soggiorno -
are requested. We would appreciate if you inform us
what documents are in your possession.

                                    HEINZ WINKLER
                                    Emigration Office

Registered.

*Application for Emigration to U.S. under the terms of the displaced persons bill.
July 23, 1949.*

ITALIAN MISSION PROCESSING CENTER
B A G N O L I

25th November 1949

TO WHOM IT MAY CONCERN:

This is to certify that Mr. MAURER WILHELM, born
on 26.5.1922 at Krakow, Poland has been according to our records
inmate of Bremen and Salzburg Nr Rome (Austria) from 6.5.1945, till
January 1948 and been inmate of Bagnoli, Pretto, Milan and Bagnoli Nr
Genoa (Italy) from January 1948 till 25th November 1949.

G. TSUCHIYANE KUBATA
Camp Director.

Certification letter. Bagnoli, Italy, processing center. 1949.

DPC-219
4-13-49

DISPLACED PERSONS COMMISSION
WASHINGTON 25, D. C.

Dear Sir or Madam:

The Displaced Persons Commission welcomes you to the United States of America.

The Congress of the United States of America has established the Displaced Persons Commission to select for immigration to this country, persons displaced as a result of World War II. Under the principles laid down by the Congress, you are among those selected.

The Congress is interested in how displaced persons fare after settling in the United States. So that the Congress may be kept informed on this matter, it requires that each person who immigrated to the United States as the head of a family or as a single person provide certain factual information.

The information is to be provided twice a year, for two years. The reporting dates are July 1 and January 1. The first report is required on the next reporting date after you have been in the country 60 or more days. Each of the reports must be in the mails to reach us by the date specified, but may be mailed as much as fifteen days earlier.

The form for reporting is provided by the Displaced Persons Commission. The form to be used will be available on May 15 for the July 1 report and on November 15 for the January 1 report. It will be available at local offices of the U. S. Immigration and Naturalization Service.

The Displaced Persons Commission wishes you every success in your new life in the United States of America.

Sincerely,

Ugo Carusi, Chairman

Edward M. O'Connor

Harry N. Rosenfield

Welcome letter from Displaced Persons Commission. Washington, D.C. 1949.

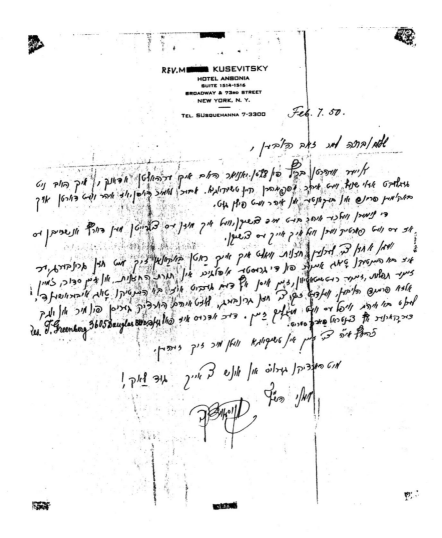

Scholarship recommendation from Cantor Moshe Kusevitsky of the famous Tlomackie Street Synagogue (The Great Synagogue). February 7, 1950

Graduation day at the Cantor's Institute of the College of Jewish Studies.
Chicago, Illinois. 1958

Cantor William Hauben at Temple Beth Am, Los Angeles, California. 1961

Cantor Hauben photographed at Temple Rodeph Sholom, Tampa, Florida. 1985

CHICAGO PUBLIC SCHOOLS

DIVISION OF

AMERICANIZATION

SECOND CERTIFICATE

This certifies that *William Houben*
has satisfactorily completed the intermediate
work in americanization and adult education
of the Chicago Public Schools and is entitled
to this Certificate.

Workmen's Circle Lyceum School

GENERAL SUPERINTENDENT OF SCHOOLS

DIRECTOR, BUREAU OF EDUCATION EXTENSION

DIRECTOR, DIVISION OF AMERICANIZATION *Vernon Bowyer*

PRESIDENT, BOARD OF EDUCATION

SECRETARY, BOARD OF EDUCATION

Chicago *June 15* 19 50

Americanization certificate. June 15, 1950.

· 74 ·

Cantor and two Bar Mitzvah boys

Överrabbin Morton H. Narrowe

Judiska Församlingen i Stockholm

Cantor Willian Hauben
4830 San José
Tampa Fla - 33629
USA

                                    August 4, 1987

Dear Cantor Hauben,

On behalf of those attending the Synagogue of the Jewish Community
of Stockholm, I want to thank you for your vendition of the difficult
Haftara Chazon on 1 August 1987. We who are distant from the centers
of Jewish life are extremely appreciative of the unique and often
unforgettable contributions to our spiritual and cultural life made
by educated and talented leaders from afar. American Jewry does a
great service by sharing people like yourself with less fortunate
congregations.

Most sincerely,

Moeton H. Narrowe
Chief Rabbi, Stockholm, Sweden

Letter from Chief Rabbi, Stockholm, Sweden. August 4, 1987.

SURVIVORS OF THE
SˑHˑOˑAˑH
VISUAL HISTORY FOUNDATION.

6 April 1998

William Hauben
4902 Bayshore Blvd
Tampa, FL 33629

Dear Mr. Hauben,

Thank you for contributing your testimony to Survivors of the Shoah Visual History Foundation. In sharing your story, you have granted future generations the opportunity to experience a direct connection with history.

Your interview will be carefully preserved as an important part of the most comprehensive library of Holocaust testimonies ever assembled. Far into the future, people will be able to see a face, hear a voice, and observe a life, so that they may listen and learn, and always remember.

Thank you for your invaluable contribution, your strength, and your generosity of spirit.

All my best,

Steven Spielberg
Chairman

Letter from Steven Spielberg acknowledging video document contributed by William Hauben for the Shoah Visual History Foundation. 1998.

PART II

Liberation at Ebensee

It was May 6, 1945, the day of liberation by the Americans—the 3rd Cavalry Group (mechanized) commanded by Colonel James H. Polk. "Crowding by the fence and listening intently, we heard them on the road below. An unfamiliar rumbling, squeaking sound of them coming up our road grew louder...two enormous tanks lumbered around the bend of our road, followed by a curious, small, open vehicle. On our side of the fence, we prisoners surged toward the locked main gate, as the tanks and the auxiliary vehicle stopped just outside...the gates somehow were opened, and we drew back to allow the roaring tanks and their small escort roll slowly into the middle of our roll call square..." (as quoted by Dutch liberated Ebensee inmate Max Garcia). Commandant Anton Ganz came out with his arms raised and a white flag in hand. He was disarmed by the first American tank patrol, and then driven away for interrogation.

Commandant Ganz did not follow the order to liquidate the 18,000 inmates, and this decision saved his life and ours. In 1972, before the Court of Menningen, Ganz admitted that two trucks loaded with land mines were sent to the tunnels on May 4, 1945, for the purpose of murdering the 18,000 remaining inmates. The days before liberation shaped the final outcome, another miracle that surpasses all others.

In the days leading up to liberation by the Americans, the SS was becoming more and more afraid of the prisoners. SS Commandant Ganz would not enter the camp alone anymore, except with a dog at his side. A leaflet had been dropped over Ebensee and its surrounding areas on April 23 by the Americans, a copy of which was smuggled into the camp by a prisoner who had worked on a detail outside the camp on that particular day. The leaflet was signed by the governments of the United States, the USSR, and Great Britain, and warned the guard troops and the Gestapo officials against the maltreatment of Prisoners of War of the allied nations. Members of the illegal organization (international camp committee) who worked in the camp hospital, and who were daily confronted with death and suffering, demanded that there should be an uprising. They questioned how long the "healthy" prisoners would remain strong enough to support such an action. With a daily death rate of 200-300 dead at Ebensee, it would become a race with time. One German political prisoner was allowed to have a radio. Members of the resistance units in the camp listened to foreign broadcasts on a daily basis to keep informed on the position of allied forces.

The international camp committee had been formed in the camp, in 1944, in preparation for the critical phase of liberation. The committee was afraid that the lives of all the prisoners would be in great danger when the Allied forces approached; they had received detailed information about the mass murders at other destruction camps in Poland, and suspected that the SS, realizing its hopeless situation, would try to kill all the prisoners in one way or another. Although weapons had been smuggled into the camp, by the time liberation came there was only a meager supply available for use by the prisoners.

Sometime in the early hours of May 5, 1945, the international camp committee learned of orders to blow up the prisoners in the tunnel that day. They invited as many prisoners as possible to take part in the resistance and asked them to refuse to go into the tunnels. At the roll call on May 5, Commandant Ganz stood before the prisoners, with SS men standing by, and addressed the prisoners as "gentlemen." Ganz's German orders were translated by one of the men into several languages, so all prisoners would understand. Ganz had ordered the prisoners to go into the tunnels, and there were prisoners' voices shouting back that they did not want to go into the tunnels. The rejection was unanimous, and beautiful. This was a revolt, and in that very moment the prisoners were no longer prisoners. In their faces, there was a look of determination, courage, self-confidence, and pure joy. I was an eager participant, as weak as I was.

Ganz was surprised. He had not expected resistance from the prisoners and seemed uncertain as to what to do. He turned toward his group of SS officers and conferred with them. He turned back to us and spoke in a trembling voice, trying to control his anger. He spoke slowly, and carefully, and said that if we didn't want to go into the tunnels we didn't have to, and that he wouldn't be responsible for the consequences; it was at our own risk. The SS men left the roll call square in an agitated and nervous state; that afternoon they left the camp for good.

The prisoners were shaking hands and hugging one another at their successful act of resistance but were still afraid. At last, the international camp committee took charge of the camp, step by step. The rage of the prisoners held back for so long was turned loose, and they broke out openly against all those who had collaborated with the SS. It was an unmerciful massacre, with about fifty-two camp functionaries killed.

At 2:50 p.m. on May 6 the Americans arrived at the main gate of Ebensee. The soldiers gaped in wonder from the top of their tanks at a mass of shrunken, ghastly scarecrows in filthy, striped rags, a reeking mass with their heads shaved except for a stripe down the middle. The soldiers stared at us and we stared back at them. The Americans had been advised by advance units that a concentration camp existed near the town of Ebensee that contained 16,000 starving political prisoners, and that the condition of the camp was pitiful. They were told that the prisoners lived in filth, and were in such a state that some felt no horror in eating their dead comrades.

Initially, the American soldiers in and on their tanks seemed afraid of us and didn't want to come down to mingle with the prisoners. It seemed to be too much for them. When one prisoner spoke up in English, the soldiers relaxed a bit.

Initiatives were taken to tour and inspect the camp, order food and medical care, and assess and ease the situation of this indescribable scene as quickly as possible. These combat veterans returned to their tanks looking sick from what they had seen.

When the International Red Cross moved in, they registered the entire prison population, and we received our Liberation Certificates signed by the American officer in charge, who was also commander of the liberated camp. Italian and Polish authorities also co-signed the document.

As soon as food was made available, there were catastrophic circumstances (caused by consuming too much food) for the half-starved prisoners. Suddenly, illnesses began to appear that caused the death of many of these weakened prisoners after the liberation. UNRRA, the 30th American Field Hospital, and the 139th evacuation Hospital arrived in Ebensee. It was a truly great effort: to see these mobile American hospital units take care of thousands of patients each day, when their maximum capacity was 800 patients, was a sight to behold. When the 30th Field Hospital arrived on May 8, there were no clothing, no housing, no food or eating utensils, yet in a very short time they were successful in reducing the death rate.

After regaining strength, the liberated prisoners returned to their home countries, partly on their own, partly with organized transports. Several delegations arrived at Ebensee waving the flags of their respective countries, and inviting the liberated prisoners to leave with them. There was a happy mood in the camp, with lots of food, music, flowers, new clothing, and famous professional comedians for entertainment. Within a few weeks the entire camp was empty. But we handful of Jewish "liberated" people had nowhere to go.[10] Liberated after so many

---

[10] 300.000 Jews survived Hitler's concentration camps-two-thirds fled to Palestine after the war, even though Jewish immigration there was illegal. Of those two-thirds, 72,000 survivors headed for the United States, another 16,000 went to Canada, 1,000 to Great Britain. The remainder stayed in Europe.

years of persecution, fear, and intolerable living conditions, and NOWHERE TO GO. We were not welcome in Poland, and we later learned that the Jewish survivors of the camps were not well tolerated, or welcome, in most European countries. At the time of liberation, my physical condition was extremely poor; I was barely able to walk. As far as I can remember, my diet to help me get back on my feet consisted of one soft-cooked egg, one glass of milk, a few crackers, and a small glass of orange juice daily. This menu was prescribed for four weeks. My stomach had shrunk so much that any more than that quantity of food would have made another statistic of me.

When I regained my strength, there was work yet to be done for our rescuers. American intelligence officers questioned those of us remaining to see who was qualified for surveillance work. I was assigned by U.S. Army intelligence to participate in such work at a nearby hospital for Prisoners of War—Germans, Poles, and Volksdeutsche. My job was to pretend that I was in a coma, and listen for anything that could be deemed classified information, and that could help the Americans. I would be taken out of the room, periodically, on the pretense that it was for x-rays, or special tests, and would then report to the Americans any information overheard in the hospital room. This work continued for several months until I was evacuated to Italy by the Jewish Brigade from Palestine.

Evacuation to Modena

About six months following liberation, we, the Jewish remnant of Ebensee, were evacuated to Modena, Italy. This evacuation was made possible by the Jewish Brigade, under British command, stationed somewhere in Italy. They had learned that about 350 Jews still remained in Ebensee, and contacted us with instructions that they would be arriving in trucks at a given time and we were to be ready to travel to Modena. After my evacuation, I served with the Jewish Brigade and worked for Israeli intelligence assisting with evacuation of survivors from Austria to Italy.

Life in Italy was quite pleasant. Our food and shelter were sponsored by the United Nations Relief & Rehabilitation Agency (UNRRA). Through the American Jewish Joint Distribution Committee (AJJDC),[11] one of the very best refugee rehabilitation agencies in the world, I learned about an audition that would take place at the Giuseppe Verdi Conservatory, in Torino, Italy. I won a scholarship in the vocal department, and studied voice and opera from 1946-1949. My training in Torino was a turning point in my musical career.

I visited Catholic cathedrals, learned Gregorian music, and the culture of the Italian liturgical music. I was able to sing in talent contests arranged by the Conservatory. It was training that I could never have gotten under ordinary circumstances. My specialty was romantic Italian songs (not opera) and I had an audience who appreciated good music and talent. I earned about ten dollars each evening I performed, for about three evenings a week. It was pocket change. My Italian name for William was Guglielmo, and they gave me the Italian-sounding name of Haubeno so that I would fit in with the crowd where I entertained.

* * *

After three years of intensive studies at the Conservatory, I took a leave of absence to develop other skills (just in case the singing did not provide a substantial enough living for me). I relocated to the small

---

[11] The AJJDC provided food and shelter for a number of worthy Jewish students living in Torino, Italy (all refugees from the camps, the forests, or Siberia). About sixty students of different specialties, such as veterinary medicine, voice, medicine, law, engineering, and art, who were studying at various universities, were entitled to live in Casa Dello Studente student hostel, at 185 Corso Moncalieri, Torino, Italy. We were like one big happy family.

northern Italian city of Ivrea, where the Organization for Rehabilitation & Training (ORT), provided opportunities for individuals to learn a trade by serving an apprenticeship at the Olivetti manufacturing facility, owned by three Jewish Olivetti brothers. The training was arranged by ORT so that we could earn a living when we emigrated to the United States, or whichever country would have us.

Olivetti produced manual and electric typewriters, adding machines, calculators, and teletype machines. In 1948, when the State of Israel was proclaimed, the Olivetti Company received an order from Israel for delivery of the first Hebrew typewriters. Because of our knowledge of the Hebrew language, our entire group was assigned to the special Hebrew typewriter division (as I recall, the initial order from Israel was for 100,000 typewriters). Prior to this time, only English or Arabic keys were used on their typewriters.

A major order also came in to Olivetti from the Polish government requesting the shipment, via special freight train, of Olivetti products to Poland. The administration was searching for a person who spoke Polish, German, and Italian, one who would accompany the train for purposes of communicating with the border guards in Italy, Germany, Austria, Czechoslovakia, and Poland. I happened to be selected because I had these qualifications. As a student, I could pass freely between all of the borders, but once I was employed by Olivetti my status changed. Olivetti arranged for a special passport for me to ensure my safe return to Italy.

When I successfully completed the delivery of freight to the capital of Warsaw, Poland, I subsequently visited Cracow, where I visited with my uncle Henryk and aunt Dziuna Staskiewicz (my uncle's Jewish name was Leopold Hauben). My aunt and uncle escaped from Wieleczka Ghetto, using papers from dead persons in the hospital, and, posing as Gentiles (living as Christians). They found employment in the city of Lublin until the liberation. My aunt worked as a domestic worker for a Wehrmacht officer, and my uncle as a forester.

Emigration to the United States

When I returned to Italy, I applied for my emigration papers. I was transferred to Grugliasco, a temporary camp at Bagnoli, Italy, near Napoli. We had to go through extensive interviews, in ten different rooms, with two weeks of processing, to be sure we were not communists or criminals. The American Joint Distribution Committee based in Milan handled all of the paperwork for us. My entire background was researched. I was finally informed by the American Emigration Office that I had been assigned case No. 94308, and that my visa to the United States was waiting for me (President Harry Truman was instrumental in arranging for 100,000 displaced persons to enter the United States after the war).

The date of my arrival in the United States was December 26, 1949. My job sponsor was the Royal Typewriter Company, but I was not particularly happy there. I happened to see an ad placed by the new U.S. branch of Olivetti in Chicago and was able to transfer to Olivetti without delay. My supervisor at Olivetti was Italian, and we were able to communicate very well. Moving to Olivetti was a very positive move for me. I had been part of their organization in Italy, before coming to the United States, and didn't have to prove myself. I was subsequently asked to take a managerial position with Olivetti. Because of my knowledge of languages, and my mastery of the mechanical requirements of the job, they realized that I was well suited for the position. For the first time in my life, I was now earning a substantial income.

Simultaneous with employment at Olivetti Typewriter Company, I registered at the Cantor's Institute of the College of Jewish Studies in Chicago. I presented a letter of recommendation from the late, world-renowned Cantor Moshe Kusevitzky (Kusevitzky had a graceful yet powerful lyric tenor voice. His recordings remain prized possessions of those who love to listen to the voices of the great cantors of the past). The way that I met Cantor Kusevitzky is an interesting story in itself.

Cantor Moshe Kusevitzky served the famous Tlomackie Street Synagogue (The Great Synagogue) for many years, in Warsaw, Poland, and miraculously survived the war in Soviet Russia. Ludovico Rocca, the Christian-Italian composer and director of the Giuseppe Verdi Conservatory, where I studied for three years in Torino, composed the very dramatic opera *Dybuk*. He spent many months listening to the famous cantors and choirs in Polish cities and small villages, where he made musical notations for the preparation of the stage setting and musical production for his opera (Ludovico Rocca's inspiration for the composition of the *Dybuk* opera came after listening to a boys'choir in one of the Jewish synagogues).

In 1936 *Dybuk* was staged for the first time, in Warsaw. At the special invitation of the composer, the famous choir of the Tlomackie Street Synagogue was invited to participate in the production. Ludovico Rocca and Cantor Kusevitzky became close friends, and M. Kipnis, the renowned composer of Jewish music, joined the team as a major advisor to the opera production. Before I departed to the United States in December of 1949, Ludovico Rocca asked me to take a gift to Cantor Kusevitzky, now living in New York, of many volumes of synagogue music that he had saved during the Nazi occupation of Italy.

While visiting with Cantor Kusevitzky in New York, I auditioned with him. He then wrote a letter of recommendation on my behalf to the head of the Cantor's Institute of the College of Jewish Studies. When I auditioned in Chicago, I was accepted with a full scholarship to the Institute, a final tribute to my formal music education that began at age fifteen. I graduated as a cantor on June 23, 1958 (my cantorial studies at the Institute were part-time, evenings and Sundays).

As with most survivors of the Holocaust, it has been very difficult and painful for me to recall my experiences during the war years, especially those memories of my dear mother, brother, and father, of blessed memory, and the loss of sixty-five extended family members. The horror, disbelief, and insecurity that survivors had to live through in the camps was a numbing experience. After a while, the fear and torment, the hunger, and having to obey orders in order to survive were all we could think about. We were devoid of emotion. This is how I *started* to write my story and, with great effort, I feel that I have brought the reader a little closer to what was really happening in my life during that incredible period of my adolescence and young adulthood. I thank G-d for my survival in this final prayer:

William Hauben

I love to know that the Lord listens to
my cry of supplication.

Because he gives me a hearing,
I will call on him all of my days.

The cords of death encompassed me,
the grave held me in its grip;
I found myself in anguish and despair.

I called on the Lord; I prayed that he would save me.

Gracious is the Lord, and kind; our God is compassionate.

The Lord protects the simple;
I was brought low and he saved me.

Be at ease once again, my soul,
for the Lord has dealt kindly with you.

He has delivered me from death,
My eyes from tears, my feet from stumbling.

I shall walk before the Lord in the land of the living.

I kept my faith even when greatly afflicted, even when
in panic I cried out: all mortals are undependable.

Psalm 116:1-11.

Afterword

Very soon after my liberation from Ebensee Concentration Camp, in Austria, I realized that I was saved from certain death by coincidence on at least five different occasions. I began to believe with all my heart, all my mind, and all my soul that it was my mission to dedicate my life to salvaging as many pre-Holocaust culture items from our destroyed generation as was possible. I felt that the only way we would be able to educate our next generation was to search for artifacts, rare books, photographs, and a variety of other documents, especially from Germany and Austria. I resolved to recover and preserve whatever I could of Jewish culture from war torn countries (*Kristallnacht*, the "Night of the Broken Glass," generated the greatest damage, when almost everything of Jewish culture was completely destroyed. Jewish books burned by day and night for weeks). I was able to accumulate a substantial number of what I call "rescue" items that had been hidden away from the Germans, and other precious material from Germany, Austria, Poland, Russia, Hungary, Rumania. Most of the original printed music and a variety of religious books are still in excellent condition. My aunt Regina Hendel, of blessed memory, was instrumental in helping to make my dream a reality.

Aunt Regina emigrated to Israel by way of Poland in 1960. She was liberated from Bergen-Belsen in 1945 and sent to a refugee camp in Sweden. From there, she went to Cracow, Poland, and then to Tel Aviv, Israel, where she opened a shop of collectibles and rare rescued books, mostly from Eastern Europe. She also had scarce Israeli and British mandate coins and medals, rare stamps, and other unique materials originating from Turkey, and Great Britain. Regina Hendel was a most generous individual who contributed many of her rare possessions to me as a gift.

My uncle Henryk Staskiewicz also possessed a large collection of items of Jewish culture that had been rescued during the war. When I visited Cracow (while still an employee of Olivetti in Italy), he invited me to look over his collection. Although it could not be classified as rescued materials I found, among other things, a recently released book (dated 1947) that documented the final trial of the notorious Amon Goeth, published by the Polish War Crimes Tribunal. It consisted of some 500 pages that included witness testimonies from both Jewish and Gentile survivors, very rare pictures from Plaszow and the trial, and examples of Goeth's handwriting. My uncle Henryk convinced me that I should have this particular book, which he considered a rare, historical document. My uncle now lives in Stockholm, Sweden, having just reached his 86th birthday.

The years since my retirement have been a most fulfilling experience for me. I maintain contact with my former students and congregation members on a regular basis and, for the past two years, have been collaborating with my associate, Marian Bruin, on developing a catalog for my rare collection detailing Jewish literary musical and religious history from Germany and Eastern Europe. The original artifacts span the 19th century through World War II. Under the auspices of The William Hauben Heritage Foundation, Inc., my collection will be exhibited at Holocaust museums in the United States, with some of the items already committed for the U.S. Holocaust Museum in Washington, D.C., for inclusion in the year 2000 exhibit, "Life Reborn." A curriculum has been developed for an educational program aimed toward young people, focusing not only on the Holocaust, but also on the preservation of Jewish life, history, and culture.

The book you now hold in your hands is the culmination of all of my dreams, all of my experiences, and I offer it to you, the reader, as your most humble servant. I am often asked, "Cantor, how have you found the power to forgive?" And I tell them that forgiveness is part of the Jewish tradition, that the people who perpetrated the crimes against our people are for the most part not around anymore. How can we blame the children and grandchildren—they should not have to share the guilt. And yet...

I have been interviewed for director Steven Spielberg's *Visual History of the Shoah* [Holocaust] project. My interview, among others, on behalf of survivors of the Shoah Visual History Foundation, will be carefully preserved on videotape as an important part of the most comprehensive library of Holocaust testimonies ever assembled, and I quote, "Far into the future, people will be able to see a face, hear a voice, and observe a life, so that they may listen and learn, and always remember." Steven Spielberg, Chairman, Survivors of the Shoah Visual History Foundation.

About the Author

Following his liberation from Ebensee Concentration Camp, William Hauben completed three years of intensive vocal studies at the Giuseppe Verdi Conservatory, in Torino, Italy, under the guidance of some of the finest voice teachers in Italy. He went on to complete his studies for the cantorate at the Cantor's Institute of the College of Jewish Studies, in Chicago, Illinois. The hazzan became affiliated with Temple Beth Am, Los Angeles, California, as associate cantor from 1958-1969. He was then invited to serve as cantor and music director at Rodeph Sholom Congregation, in Tampa, Florida, from 1969-1990. Among his list of accomplishments, Cantor Hauben is best known for creating Rodeph Sholom's Annual Music Festival, which grew to take national honors, to attract world-renowned performers from the Metropolitan Opera, and others. The festival was recognized as the highlight of Jewish cultural programs in the Tampa Bay area. Because of Cantor Hauben's wide range of knowledge, and his large collection of Jewish repertoire (the largest library in all of central Florida), his choir was able to present the classic composers of the 19th century, and their influence on 20th century Jewish composers representing many different countries. His services reflected the "harmony of the world." Cantor Hauben had become what one congregant called "an institution in his own right...and his warmth still draws happiness from those around him."

The cantor's kind and devoted wife, Brina, of blessed memory, passed away in recent years and did not live to see the results of all her husband's efforts on behalf of preservation of Jewish culture. His son Sheldon, and beautiful wife, Mindy, continue to be a joy and comfort to William Hauben in his retirement years.

Since his retirement, William Hauben has served as director of American-Israeli Youth Programs for the Tampa Bay region of the Jewish National Fund. He is widely known for his work with youth in the community.

Resources

To attempt to recall events in my life that occurred more than fifty-five years ago taxes the imagination, a task that I could not have accomplished without the support system offered by the following publications and sources: *A Nightmare in History,* by Miriam Chaiken; *The Holocaust,* by Jack R. Fischel; *The War Against the Jews,* by Lucy S. Dawidowicz; *The Holocaust:* Memories, Research, References, Edited by Robert Hauptman & Susan Hubbs Motin; *Schindler's List,* by Thomas Keneally; *The Trial of Amon Goeth,* by Polish War Crimes Tribunal; Yad Vashem Museum, Jerusalem, Israel; *The World Book Encyclopedia,* by World Book, Inc.; *Encyclopedia Brittanica,* by Grolier, Inc.; *Collier's Encyclopedia,* MacMillan Educational Company; *Krakow Ghetto & the Plaszow Camp Remembered,* by Malvina Graf; *Concentration Camp Ebensee:* Sub Camp of Mauthausen, Translated by Max A. Garcia; *The Cantors:* Gifted Voices Remembered, by Bea Kraus.

The William Hauben Heritage Foundation, Inc.

Collection Catalog

Contents

Bibles of the World

No.	Title	Date	Publisher
1B	Biblia Hebraica—Tenach	1849	
2B	Feast New Year	1918	Hebrew Publ. Co.
3B	Medrash Thilim	1947	Om Publ. Co.
4B	Hebrew Union College Annual	1904	Hebrew Union College, Cincinnati
5B	We Celebrate	1979 ed	J.S. Paluch Co., Chicago
6B	The Holy Bible-Old & New Testament	1979	Church of Jesus Christ
7B	Intro. Hebrew Method	1885	Arca Seminary, Salt Lake City Charles Scribners' Sons, N.Y.
8B	The Dead Sea Scrolls, After 40 Years	1990	Biblical Arch. Soc., Washington, DC
9B	Judaism and Christianity	1968	W.B. Silverman, Behrman House
10B	Tanach & New Testament	1956	Rev. O. Roberts
11B	A Book of Jewish Thought	1913	Jewish Welfare Bd., N.Y.
12B	The Koran	1956	Betty Radice, London
13B	Between the Testaments	1960	Fortress Press, Philadelphia
14B	Religious Life & Communities	1974	Keter Publ. House, Jerusalem
15B	Where Judaism Differed	1957	A.H. Silver, Jewish Publ. Soc., Philadelphia

16B	Music of the Jews	1967	A.S. Barnes, N.J.
17B	A Primer of Hebrew	1903	C. Scribners' & Sons
18B	Additional Jehovah's Witness Collection—100 Pamphlets		
19B	Dictionary of the Bible— Antiquities, Biography, Geography, Natural History	1918 ed	Fleming H. Revell Co., N.Y., Chicago, Toronto; William Smith, Illus.; Classical Examiner of Univ. of London

Replica Haggadoth

No.	Title	Date	Publisher
1H	Amsterdam Haggadah	1695	Orphan Hospital Ward of Israel
2H	Matteh Aharon	1710	Orphan Hospital Ward of Israel
3H	Venice Haggadah	1716	Diskin Orphan Home of Israel
4H	Leipnik Darmstadt	1733	H.M. Spira Printing, U.S.A.
5H	Tel-Aviv Haggadah	1771	Orphan Hospital Ward of Israel
6H	Trieste Haggadah	1864	Colomro Coen, Editor
7H	Haggadah of B'Ene Israel of India	1867	Orphan Hospital Ward of Israel
8H	Graziano Haggadah	1800	Jewish Library of J. TH. Jemi of America
9H	Passover Haggadah		K'Tav Publ. Co., N.Y.
10H-A	Passover Haggadah with Music	1912	Hebrew Publ. Co., N.Y.
10H-B	The Exodus Haggadah: A Celebration		United Jewish Appeal Rabbinic Cabinet
11H	Union Haggadah		Union of Hebrew Congregations, Cincinnati
4XN	Offenbach Haggadah	1722	The Diskin Orphan Home of Israel
5XN	Lipnik Rosent Haliana Haggadah	1738	Orphan Hospital Ward of Israel
6XN	Sulzbach Haggadah	1755	The Diskin Orphan Home of Israel
14H	Presburg Haggadah	1760	The Orphan Home of Israel

7XN	Babad Haggadah	1760	The Diskin Orphan Home of Israel
9XN	Kalsuhe Haggadah	1796	The Diskin Orphan Home of Israel
10XN	The Livorno Haggadah	1825	The Diskin Orphan Home of Israel
12H	Libreria Castellano Haggadoth		Libreria Editora S'Sigal, Buenos Aires
8XN	Hamburg Haggadah	1796	The Diskin Orphan Home of Israel
13H	Wandsberg Haggadah	1733	The Orphan Home of Israel
3XN	Openheim Haggadah	1719	Amsterdam, Holland
11XN	The Hanover Haggadah	1861	The Diskin Orphan Home of Israel

Judaica Rescue Items-Austria and Germany

No.	Name	Date	Publisher/Source
1G	Stamp for Kosher Soap	1936	Berlin
2G	Havdalah Box	1937	Berlin
3G	Etrog Box	1938	Berlin
4G	Historia Welfgeshichte	1815-1851	Stuttgart, Berlin, Leipzig; Austria
5G	High Holy Day Mahzor-First Day	1907	J. Schlesinger, Vienna, Austria
6G	High Holy Day Mahzor-Second Day (Translated into Yiddush with Rashi script - Rare)	1907	J. Schlesinger, Vienna, Austria
7G	Daily Prayers-Custom, German, Polish Jews	1927	Austria
8G	Midrash Rabot Commentary Hatal "Gishmey"	1897	Lewenberger, M. Rodelheim
9G	Prayer Book: Slichot Yotzrot. Hoshanoth & Hagadah for Passover	1833	J. Schlesinger, Vienna, Austria
10G	Prayer Book: Festivals (with English translations)	1900	J. Schlesinger, Vienna, Austria
11G	Pentateuch: B'reyshith & Prayer Book	1906	Lewenberger, M. Rodelheim
12G	Pentateuch: Sh'moth & Prayer Book	1906	Lewenberger, M. Rodelheim
13G	Pentateuch: Vayikrah Prayer Book	1906	Lewenberger, M. Rodelheim

14G	Pentateuch: Bamidbar Prayer Book	1906	Lewenberger, M. Rodelheim
15G	Pentateuch: D'Varim Prayer Book	1906	Lewenberger, M. Rodelheim
16G	Gesange "Thora"	1891	Shaffhausen, Germany
17G	Gtzvi Leket-A Combination of a Variety of Prayers	1877	L. Tzvi Rodelheim, Germany
18G	"Toldoth Hanginah Haivrith" (Modes and Trops)—Rare Material		Berlin, Dvir, Tel-Aviv
19G	Pentateuch: Vayikrah & Prayer Book	1867	J. Schlesinger, Vienna, Austria
20G	Judishe Volkslieder by Janet Ruskin (Personal signature of Janot S. Ruskin) "Hatikvah"	1922	Berlin

Judaica Rescue Items-Poland, Russia, U.S.A.

No.	Name	Date	Author	Country
2E	D'Varim—#5	1897	Pietrokoof	Poland
3E	Bamidbar—#4	1897	Pietrokoof	Poland
4E	Machzor—Pesach III	1878	P. Balavan	Poland
5E	Machzor—Rosh Hashana I	1878	P. Balavan	Poland
6E	Machzor—Yom Kippur II	1878	P. Balavan	Poland
7E	Machzor for Sukkoth IV	1878	P. Balavan	Poland
8E	Neviim Uksuvim (Prophets Writing)	1867	J. Goldman	Poland
9E	80 Folks Lieder (in Yiddish)	1920(?)	M. Kipnis	Poland
10E	Machzor-Rosh Hashana & Yom Kippur	1889		Poland
11E	Thilim	1861	Sikora, Milner	Poland
12E	Bamidbar—#4	1875		Poland
13E	Vayikrah—#3	1875		Poland
14E	M'Norath Hamaor with Yiddush translation	1861		Poland
15E	Yhoshua, Shoftim Sh'muel	1862		Poland
16E	Choszen Mishpot	1824		Poland
17E	Machzor—Rosh Hashana & Yom Kippur	1836		Poland
18E	Siftei R'Nanot Hashalem	1828	J. Cederbaum	Poland
19E	Yidishe Volkslieder	1912	Int. Library Publ.	New York

20E	T'Hilim & Prayer Book	1865		Poland
21E	Code of Jewish Law (Shlchan Aruch)	1927	Rabel, Caro Hebrew Publ. Co.	New York
22E	A Hurrian Cult Song	1918 Copyright ca 1400	D. Kilmer Drafkorn	
23E	Shalom Aleychem (original text in Yiddush)	1918 Copyright 1886	Olga Rabinowitz	New York
24E	History of the Jews	1902	Prof. H. Gratz, Jewish Publ. Society of America	Philadelphia
25E	Repertoire Due Violiniste (Music Theory in Russian)	1907		Russia
28E	Book of Children's Plays	1922	Ch. Kaplan	Russia
29E	The Olders Book of Chumash Shir Hashirim: Ruth, Koheleth, Ester, Eicha, Haftaroth	1782		Russia
30E	Music Teacher in Yiddush (Elementary Theory of Music)	1928	M. Posner	New York

William Hauben

Holocaust Medals, Coins, Etc.

No.	Description	Date	Source
1MC	From Holocaust to Rebirth	1981	Israel State Medal
2MC	Concentration Camp, Silver Medal	1981	Israel State Medal
3MC	Concentration Camp, Bronze Medal	1942-1992	Israel State Medal
4MC	State Medal in Memory of Polish Jewry		Israel State Medal
5MC	"Let My People Go" (special commemorative coin—silver, uncircluated)		Israel Government Coins & Medal Corp.—Bank of Israel
6MC	U.S. Holocaust Memorial Museum Tape (Miles Lerman—Narrator)		U.S. Holocaust Memorial Museum, Washington, DC
7MC	9 First Day Cover Envelopes— Prisoners in Concentration Camp Uniforms	4/27/65	Jerusalem
8MC	"Let My People Go—We Are Here" (10 lb. silver coin & special bronze medal)	1971	Jerusalem
9MC	Hanukah Menorah (handmade from Poland—used in Plaszow Concentration Camp)	1943-1944	Plaszow, Poland

Holocaust Photos

No.	Description	Credit	Source
1HP	Auschwitz, A Crime Against Mankind	K. Amolwn, T. Swiebocka	Auschwitz State Museum, Poland (1991)
2HP	Anne Frank	Anne Frank Stichtng	Amsterdam (1985)
3HP	A Day in the Warsaw Ghetto	Dr. Yitzhak Arad	Yad Vashem Israel (1988)
4HP	The Children We Remember	Abells Chana Byers	Kar-Ben Copies, Inc., U.S.A.
5HP	The Marshall Cavendish Illustrated Encyclopedia of WWII, Vol. 1		Marshall Cavendish Corp., N.Y.
6HP	WWII—A 50th Anniversary History	Donald Salisbury, D. Hutter	H. Holt & Co., N.Y.
7HP	The Liberators, Vol. 1 Liberation Day		Center for Holocaust Studies Documentation, N.Y.
8HP	The Holocaust—Martyrs and Heroes Remembrance Authority		Yad Vashem, Israel (1977)
9HP	U.S. GIs See Nazi Death Camp		Tampa Tribune (2/21/82)
10HP	21 Pictures of Himmler's Activities		Time Life Books, Inc.

Holocaust Books

No.	Title	Author	Publisher
1HB	Commandant of Auschwitz		The World Publishing Co., N.Y.
2HB	Treblinka	J.F. Steiner	Simon & Schuster, N.Y.
3HB	The Holocaust	Nora Levin	T.Y. Crowell Co., N.Y.
4HB	The War Against the Jews	Lucy S. Dawidowicz	Holt, Rinehart & Winston, N.Y.
5HB	The Holocaust Kingdom	A. Donat	Holocaust Library, N.Y.
6HB	The Fighting Ghettos	M. Barkai	J.B. Lippingott Co., Philadelphia
7HB	Hitler's War Against the Jews	D.A. Altshuler	Behrman House Inc., N.Y.
8HB	The Holocaust (A History of the Jews of Europe During WWII)	Martin Gilbert	Henry Holt Co., N.Y.
9HB	SS and Gestapo	Roger Manvell	
10HB	The Death Brigade	Leon Weliczer Wells	Holocaust Library, N.Y.
11HB	The Rise & Fall of Adolph Hitler	William L. Shirer	Scholastic Book Service, N.Y.
12HB	The Death Camp Treblinka	A. Donat	Holocaust Library, N.Y.
13HB	Hitler: A Study of Tyranny	A. Bullock	FitzHenry & Whiteside, Toronto
14HB	Eichman in Jerusalem	H. Arent	The MacMillan Co. of Canada

15HB	Liliana's Journal-Warsaw 1939-1945	L. Zuker Bujanowska	The Dial Press
16HB	Escape from Warsaw	I. Serraillier	Scholastic Book Service, N.Y.
17HB	The Secret Press in Nazi Europe	I. Kowalski	Shengold Publ. Co., N.Y.
18HB	Secrets and Spies		Readers Digest Assoc., Pleasantville, N.Y.
19HB	Mila 18	Leon Uris	Doubleday, N.Y.
20HB	The Holocaust: A History of Courage and Resistance	B. Stadler	Behrman House, Inc., N.Y.
21HB	Uprising in the Warsaw Ghetto	Ben Mark	Schocken Books, N.Y.
22HB	I Cannot Forgive	R. Brba; A Besic	Grove Press, Inc., N.Y.
23HB	Battle for Berlin	E.F. Ziemke	Ballantine Books, N.Y.
24HB	Holocaust		Encyclopedia Judaica Keter Books, Jerusalem
25HB	Eichman's Inferno	Dr. M. Nyiszli	Fawcett Publ. Inc., Greenwich, CT
26HB	The Case Against Adolf Eichman	H. Zeiger	New American Library, N.Y.
27HB	The Scourge of the Swastica	L. Russell	Philosophical Library, Inc., N.Y.
28HB	Never To Forget	M. Meltzer	Dell Publ. Co., N.Y.
29HB	Hasidic Tales of the Holocaust	Y. Ellach	Avon Books, N.Y.
30HB	I Am Rosemarie	M.D. Moskin	Scholastic Book Service
31HB	They Fought Back	Yuri Suhl	Schocken Books, N.Y.

No.	Title	Author	Publisher

(Photocopies of Publications)

1HBX — Concentration Camp Ebense (Subcamp of Mauthausen) — M. Garcia, translator — Archives, Vienna, Austria

2HBX — Dachau Concentration Camp (additional 50 books available based on Holocaust material) — Carl Koch

Jewish Theater Music-First Day Covers

No.	Composition	Date	Composer	Publisher
1M	Birchas Cohanim	1899	Rev. Joachim Kurantmann	K. Rabinowitz, N.Y.
2M	Beth David	1901	Samuel Roll	Hebrew Publ. Co., Brooklyn, N.Y.
3M	The Wandering Jew	1902	A. Goldfaden	S. Schenker, N.Y.
4M	Mizmor L'David	1903	J. Brody	Hebrew Publ. Co., Brooklyn, N.Y.
5M	Noch A Bisel Noch	1903	M.J. Rubinstein	A. Teres, N.Y.
6M	Soll Men's Uebergehn	1905	S. Smulewitz	A. Goldberg, N.Y.
7M	Mameniu Koif Mir Dos	1906	S. Mogulesko	S. Schenker, N.Y.
8M	Man Und Weib	1906	S. Mogulesko/ L. Friedsel	Hebrew Publ. Co., Brooklyn, N.Y.
9M	In 100 Yohr Arim	1909	J.M. Rumshinsky	A. Teres, N.Y.
10M	A Mames Verth	1909	Solomon Small	A. Teres, N.Y.
11M	The Poilisher Jew	1910	Perlmutter & Wohl	Hebrew Publ. Co., N.Y.
12M	Dos Boimele	1911	A. Goldfaden/ Rumshinsky	Hebrew Publ. Co., N.Y.
13M	Meidels Cholem	1912	Solomon Smulewitz	Hebrew Publ. Co., N.Y.

14M	Rachmono D'One	1912	Leo Loew Photo-Cantor Sirota	Hebrew Publ. Co., N.Y.
15M	Chantshe in America	1913	J.M. Rumshinsky	Hebrew Publ. Co., N.Y.
16M	Mutter Und Kind	1914	J.M. Rumshinsky	Hebrew Publ. Co., N.Y.
17M	A Brivele Von Chosen	1915	D. Meyerowitz	Hebrew Publ. Co., N.Y.
18M	Remember Mother's Tears	1915	K. Liptzin	A. Teres, N.Y.
19M	Bruder Isralik (in Zion)	1916	Henry Russotto	Hebrew Publ. Co., N.Y.
20M	Uptown Downtown	1916	J.M. Rumshinsky	Hebrew Publ. Co., N.Y.
21M	Zubrochene Fiedele	1916	J.M. Rumshinsky	Hebrew Publ. Co., N.Y.
22M	Dos Hupe Kleyd	1916	S. Secunda	Hebrew Publ. Co., N.Y.
23M	Rusland's Freihets Lied	1917	J.M. Rumshinsky	Hebrew Publ. Co., N.Y.
24M	A Chaver in Leben	1917	H.A. Russotto	Hebrew Publ. Co., N.Y.
25M	National Spirit	1917	J. Weinstock	Jos. P. Katz, N.Y.
26M	Mother Dear	1917	Frank J. Rowinski	Whitmore Music, N.Y.
27M	Mazel Tov	1917	J.M. Rumshinsky	Hebrew Publ. Co., N.Y.
28M	A Folk Ohn A Heim	1921	Solomon Smulewitz	A. Teres, N.Y.
29M	Mein Leebster Friend is Mein Mameniu	1921	Wohl	A. Teres, N.Y.

No.	Composition	Date	Composer	Publisher
30M	Motkie Fin Slobotkie	1922	Morris Rund	J&J Kammen, N.Y.
31M	Fohrn Yidn Fohrn Goyim	1938	T. Greenberg	Metro Music Co., N.Y.
32M	A Shtim Fun Vaitn	1938	T. Greenberg	Metro Music Co., N.Y.
33M	Ich Weis Nit Vi Me Tites	1943	Sholom Secunda	Metro Music Co., N.Y.

Original Jewish Music-Germany

No.	Composition	Date	Composer	Publisher
1GM	Fear Not Ye Israel	1889	G. Shirmer	Munich
2GM	5 Judische Lieder	1911	G. Grad	Kovno
2GMX	Aus-Und Einheben Der Thora	1904	Herman Zivi	Leipzig
3GM	Judishes Volkslied Land Von Suser	1905	J. Schonberg	Berlin
4GM	Dos Gebet (Solo/Violin/Piano)	1911	Janot S. Rusk	Berlin
5GM	A Brivele Der Mamen (Solo/Violin/ Piano)	1917	Janot S. Rusk	Hatikva, Berlin
6GM	Lieder Des Ghettos (Solo/Piano)	1911	J. Dymont	Louis Lamm, Berlin
7GM	Lied Fun Gesoyme (Solo/Piano)	1914	L. Saminsky	St. Petersburg, Russia
8GMX	Dos Tojrele (Solo/Piano)	1916	J. Roskin	Hatikva, Berlin
8GM	A "Nachtiger Tog" (Solo/Piano)	1917	J. Roskin, M. Lebenheim	Berlin
9GM	11 Judish Lieder (Solo/Piano)	1917	J. Roskin	Halensee, Berlin
9GMI	Ballade Vom Rebbe Und Die Chasidim	1917	B. Zepler	Berlin
9GMII	Das Lied Vom Voegele (Solo/Piano)	1918	B. Zepler	Berlin
10GM	Al Tal Wal Matar (Solo/Piano)	1918	J. Roskin	Lebenheim, Berlin

11GM	Juddishe Volkslieder (Solo/Piano)	1919	Arno Nadel	Freud, Berlin
12GM	Balabuste Leben (Solo/Piano)	1919	J. Roskin	Hallendel, Berlin
13GM	Mein Shifele (Solo/Piano)	1920	B. Grossman	Hallendel, Berlin
14GM	Dos Heilige Rikudl (Solo/Piano)	1917	J. Roskin	Hallendel, Berlin
15GM	Der Rebbe Hot Geheisen (Solo/Piano)	1919	J. Roskin	Hallendel, Berlin
16GM	Freitung of Der Nacht (Solo/Piano)	1919	J. Roskin	Hallendel, Berlin
17GM	Die Bajke (Volkslied) (Solo/Piano)	1920	J. Roskin	Lebenheim, Berlin
18GM	Leig Ich Mein Kepele (Solo/Piano)	1920	J. Roskin	Lebenheim, Berlin
19GM	Swei Kieder a) Ruth b) Boas	1923	J. Gladstein	Yuval, Berlin
20GM	In Cheder (Solo/Piano)	1923	M. Milner	Yuval, Berlin
21GM	Zwei Duette (Solo/Piano)	1929	J. Engel	Moscow, Leipzig
22GM	Ma Tovu (Liturgical) (Solo/Piano)	1930	J.B. Jakubow	Berlin
23GM	A Brievele Der Mame	1938		

Jewish Theater Music

No.	Composition	Date	Composer	Publisher
1ME	David Violin (Voice/Violin/Piano)	1898	H. Russotto	Hebrew Publ. Co.
2ME	B'Rosh Hashono (Voice/Violin/Piano)	1899	J. Kruantman	Hebrew Publ. Co.
3ME	My Mother's Wedding Gown	1900	J. Goldstein	Trio Press, Inc.
4ME	A Brivele Zu Gott	1902	M. Posner	Mazin & Co., London
5ME	Sisi Wesimchi (Violin/Piano)	1903	L. Friedsell	T. Lohr, N.Y.
6ME	In Hundred Year Arim	1904	J. Rumshinsky	A. Teres, N.Y.
7ME	Isrulik Kim Aheim (Solo Piano)	1904	D. Myerowitz	T. Lohr, N.Y.
8ME	Weyiten L'Cho (Violin/Piano)	1904	J. Rumshinsky	T. Lohr, N.Y.
9ME	Chasene Huben (Solo Piano)	1904	D. Myerowitz	T. Lohr, N.Y.
10ME	Seder Nacht (Solo Piano)	1904	L. Friedsell	T. Lohr, N.Y.
11ME	Yiskor (From Opera Kol Nidre)	1906	L. Friedsell	Hebrew Publ. Co.
12ME	Shenk A Neduwe (Solo Piano)	1906	Perlmutter & Wohl	Hebrew Publ. Co.
13ME	Ma Tovu (Liturgical) (Solo Piano)	1906	S. Baum	
14ME	Kadish (Liturgical) (Solo Violin/Piano)	1906	Friedsel's	Hebrew Publ. Co.
15ME	Eil Molei Rachamim (Solo Piano)	1906	Friedsel's	Hebrew Publ. Co.

16ME	Shabes Koidesh (Solo Piano)	1906	O. Motzan	S. Shenker, N.Y.
17ME	Eili Eili Solo (Solo/Piano)	1907	W. Fisher	Oliver Co., Boston
18ME	A Brivele Der Mame (Solo/Piano)	1907	S. Smulewitz	N.Y.
19ME	Eili Eli Lomo Azavtoni (Solo/Piano)	1907	H. Russotto	Hebrew Publ. Co.
20ME	M'Nucho W'Simcho (Solo/Piano)	1907	H. Russotto	Hebrew Publ. Co.
21ME	Choson Kale Mazol Tov (Solo/Piano)	1909	S. Mogulesko	Hebrew Publ. Co.
22ME	Weyiten L'Cho (Solo/Piano)	1909	J. Rumshinsky	T. Lohr, N.Y.
23ME	Men Wet Dir Nit... (Solo/Piano)	1909	J. Drody	Hebrew Publ. Co.
24ME	Oi Oi Die Weiber (Solo/Piano)	1909	R. Doctor	S. Shenker, N.Y.
25MEX	Cheszboyn Zedek (Piano Solo)	1910	L. Low	
25ME	Ach Hemri Klap (Solo/Piano)	1910	A. Bernstein	Wilno, Poland
26ME	Al Tashlichenu (Solo/Piano)	1910	S. Smulewitz	A. Teres, N.Y.
27ME	The Daughters of Zion	1911	H. Goldfaden	S. Shenker, N.Y.
28ME	Eli Eli (Solo/Piano)	1911	R.H. Zagler	S. Shenker, N.Y.
29ME	A Mother's Prayer (Solo/Piano)	1912	H. Altman	S. Shenker, N.Y.
30ME	Rachil "La Joive" (Solo/Piano)	1912	J.M. Halevy; Rumshinsky	Hebrew Publ. Co.
31ME	Das Shaifele (Solo/Piano)	1913	B. Thomashefsky	A. Teres, N.Y.
32ME	A Mames Verth (Solo/Piano)	1913	S. Small	A. Teres, N.Y.

No.	Composition	Date	Composer	Publisher
33ME	A Yuhr Noch Der Chassene	1913	I. Reingold	S. Shenker, N.Y.
34ME	A Glezele L'Chayim	1913	J. Rumshinsky	Hebrew Publ. Co.
35ME	Das Shaifele (Solo/Piano)	1913	B. Tohashefsky	A. Teres, N.Y.
36ME	The Ancient Harp (Solo/Piano)	1915	H. Lefkowitz	J.P. Katz, N.Y.
37ME	Meben Sol Columbus (Solo/Piano)	1915	Perlmutter & Wohl	A. Teres, N.Y.
38ME	Alain in Weg (Solo/Piano)	1915	N.L. Saslavsky	J.P. Katz, N.Y.
39ME	Ich Benk Tzurik A Heim (Solo/Piano)	1915	J.M. Runshinsky	A. Teres, N.Y.
40ME	Yisrael Yetz Is De Zait (Solo/Piano)	1917	H.A. Russotto	Hebrew Publ. Co.
41ME	Elijah The Prophet (Solo/Piano)	1917	H. Lefkowitz	J.P. Katz, N.Y.
42ME	Hamavdil (Solo/Piano)	1917	D. Myerowitz	Hebrew Publ. Co.
43ME	Rosh Chodesh Benschen (Liturgical) (Solo/Piano)	1917	J. Rosenblatt	Hebrew Publ. Co.
44ME	A Kind Un A Heim (Solo/Piano)	1918	I. Lillian	A. Teres, N.Y.
45MEX	Klip Klapp (Solo/Piano)	1918	A. Nadel; J. Ruskin	
45ME	Sha Sha Der Rabi Gait (Solo/Piano)	1918	A. Rosenstein	S. Shapiro, N.Y.
46ME	Meyrke My Son (Solo/Piano)	1919	M. Persin	J.P. Katz, N.Y.
47ME	A. Heim, A Heim (Solo/Piano)	1919	D. Meyrowitz	J. Kammen, N.Y.
48ME	Jankale (Solo/Piano)	1919	M. Picon	J. Kalich, N.Y.
49ME		1920		

No.	Composition	Date	Composer	Publisher
50ME		1920		
51ME	A Chant for Sabbath Night	1920	Max Persin	J.P. Katz, N.Y.
52ME	Die Novion	1920	Perlmutter & Wohl	Hebrew Publ. Co.
53ME	Eli Eli	1920	J. & J. Kammon	J.&J. Kammon, N.Y.
54ME	Vikhozhoo Odin Ya Na Donegoo	1921	L. Friedsell	Hebrew Publ. Co.
55ME	Ahin, Ahin	1921	L. Low	United Hebrew Choral Society
56ME	A Malech Veint and Yamen Roi Shel	1921	Peretz Hirshbein	J.P. Katz, N.Y.
57ME	Beim Tel Chol	1921	N. Saslausky	Intl. Library Publ. Co., N.Y.
58ME	Otzenmai. . .		Theodor Fuchs	Bucharest
59ME	Twilight Shadows	1909	J.S. Deutsch	A. Teres, N.Y.
60ME	A Klein Melamodil		N. Grabovsky	Metro Music, N.Y.
61ME	Doina Roumanian Melody	1920	Henry A. Russotto	S. Schenker, N.Y.
62ME	Dus Tolesel	1921	Pperlmutter & Wohl	Metro Music, N.Y.
63ME	A Din Toire Mit Got	1921	Leo Low	J. P. Katz, N.Y.
63MEa	A Din Toire Mit got	1921	Leo Low	Zemachsohn Music Co., N.Y.
64ME	Dem Rebens Nigen	1921	L. Friedsell	Hebrew Publ. Co., N.Y
65ME	Alone (Aline)	1922	M. Gelbart	J. P. Katz, N.Y.
66ME	Ich Bin A Boarder By Mein Weib	1922	Rubin Doctor	A. Teres Co., N.Y.
67ME	Shoifer Shel Moshiach	1923	A. Goldfaden	Hebrew Publ. Co., N.Y

68ME	A Collection of Six Popular Songs	1924	Ed. by Jos. Kammen	Kammen Music, N.Y.
69ME	Al Cheit	1924	Ch. Kotvlansky	J. P. Katz, N.Y.
70ME	A Chasendl Oif Shabes	1925	William Scher	S. Schenker, N.Y.
71ME	The New Generation	1926	S. Chesney	Chesney Music, N.Y.
72ME	A Yid Zu Zein Is Gut	1926	S. Chesney	Chesney Music, N.Y.
73ME	Menashe (A Problem)	1928	Henry Lefkowitch	Metro Music Co, N.Y.
74ME	Teiku	1929	Leo Low	Metro Music Co. N.Y.
75ME	Mazel In Liebe (Lucky In Love)	1929	A. Olshanetzky	National Theater, N.Y.
76ME	Yismechu	1930	S. Gozinsky	Metro Music Co., N.Y.
77ME	Warsze (Warsaw)	1931	J. Rumshinsky	Metro Music Co., N.Y.
78ME	Mein Shtetele Belz	1931	A. Olshanetzky	Kammen Music, N.Y.
79ME	Di Bobe	1932	S. Alman	London Music, Engl.
80ME	Got Is Gerecht	1932	S. Alman	London Music, Engl.
81ME	Bum-da-Lida	1932	J. Lengyel	
82ME	Papirosen	1932	H. Jablokoff	Kammen Music, N.Y.
83ME	I Love You Much Too Much	1934	A. Olshanetzky	Metro Music Co., N.Y.
84ME	Tchik Tchan Tchu	1934	M. Gelbart	M. Gelbart, N.Y.
85ME	When I Have Sung My Songs	1934	E. Charles	G. Shrimer, N.Y.

Orchestral Arrangements

No.	Title	Arranged For	Composer/Arranger

Yom Haatzmaut (7 Instruments)

No.	Title	Arranged For	Composer/Arranger
A	Shalom & Hadegel	Solo/Orchestra	William Hauben/Hilton Jones
B	Am Yisrael Chai	Solo/Orchestra	William Hauben/Hilton Jones
C	Hiney Ma Tov	Solo/Piano/Orchestra	William Hauben/Hilton Jones
D	Yom Huledeth	Solo/Piano/Orchestra	William Hauben/Hilton Jones
E	Naale L'Rushalayim	Solo/Piano/Orchestra	William Hauben/Hilton Jones

Israeli Music Festival

No.	Title	Arranged For	Composer/Arranger
1	Ki Mitziyon (Torah dance)	Solo/Piano/Orchestra	Max Kelfman
2	G-d Bless the State of Israel	Solo/Piano/Orchestra	M. Kopita
3	Sh'ma Yisrael	Solo/Piano/Orchestra	S. Carlebach
4	Y'Rushalayim Shel Zahav	Solo/Piano/Orchestra	N. Shemer
5	Im Eshkachech Y'Rushalayim	Solo/Piano/Orchestra	B. Selberberg
6	Oseh Shalom	Solo/Piano/Orchestra	Israeli Festival
7	Or Chadash	Solo/Piano/Orchestra	Israeli Festival
8	B'nai Vet'cha	Solo/Piano/Orchestra	Israeli Festival

9	Od Yishama & Salute to Israel	Solo/Piano/Orchestra	S. Carlebach, J. Einberg
10	Shir Hapalmach	Solo/Piano/Orchestra	Israeli Festival
11	Kumah Echa (2 versions)	Solo/Piano/Orchestra	Israeli Festival
12	V'Haeir Einenu	Solo/Piano/Orchestra	S. Carlebach
13	Sisu V'Simchu	Solo/Piano/Orchestra	Moditz Version
14	Erev Shel Shoshanim	Solo/Piano/Orchestra	Y. Hadar
15	Hanevel V'Chinor	Solo	M. Helfman
15X	Hebrew Melody	Choir/Orchestra	Max Bruch
16	Havah Neytze B'Machol	Solo/Orchestra	

Liturgical

17	Hayom Harat Olam	Solo/Piano/Orchestra	S. Silverman
18	Moadim L'Simcha (festival hymn)	Solo/Piano/Orchestra	J. Leonard
19	Maoz Tzur	Solo/Piano/Orchestra	
20	Mizmor Shir Chanukah	Solo/Piano/Orchestra	
21	Chatzi Kaddish	Solo/Flute/Cello/Choir	
22	S'u Shirim	Solo/Flute/Choir/Orchestra	E. Kirshner
23	Shecheheyanu	Solo/Choir/Orchestra	T. Greenberg
24	Haleluyah Psalm 150	Solo/Choir/Orchestra	I. Lewandowski
25	Hatikvah	Solo/Choir/Orchestra	I. Imber

No.	Title	Arranged For	Composer/Arranger

Miscellaneous

No.	Title	Arranged For	Composer/Arranger
26	Silent Devotion	Chamber Orchestra	M. Castelnuovo-Tedesco
27	Tov L'Hodoth	Choir/String Orchestra	F. Shubert
28	Exodus	Choir/Full Orchestra	Ernest Gold
29	Suite of Hebrew Themes	Special for String Orchestra	G. Berres
30	Suite of Jewish Themes	Special for String Orchestra	G. Berres
31	"Hora"	Violin Solo/String Orchestra	M. Lavry
32	Tief In Weldele	Violin Solo/Piano	L. Low
33	Reb Dovid'L	Solo/Choir/Orchestra	L. Low
34	Az Der Rebbe Elimelech		L. Low

Liturgical

No.	Title	Arranged For	Composer/Arranger
35	Rosh Hashana, Yom Kippur, Succoth	String Quartet	J. Weinberg
36	Concerto Gross	String Orchestra/Piano Obligato	E. Bloch
37	"Ayech"	Solo Tenor or Soprano/Violin/Piano	S. Alman
38	3 Hasidic Dances	Full Orchestra	L. Stein
39	Hebrew Suite	Full Orchestra	J. Chajes
40	Jerusalem Concerto (1967, copyright 1968)	Piano/Orchestra	W. Gunther-Spr(
41	V'Shamru	Solo/String Orchestra	L. Lissek
42	V'Shamru	Solo/String Orchestra	J. Lengyel

British Mandate-Palestine

No.	Name	Date	Publisher/Source
1BM	10 Varieties of Music—Postcards		Palestine, J.N.F. Jerusalem
2BM	10 Varieties of Music—Postcards		Palestine, J.N.F. Jerusalem
3BM	United Nations Gold Plated Medal with President Harry Truman	1947	Rabbi A.H. Silver, representing J. Agency
4BM	Collection of 6 Authentic Jewish Coins	135 B.C.E.	Museum of Israel, Tel Aviv
5BM	7 Historic Jewish Coins (Replica)		
6BM	Complete Uncirculated Mill Set	1927	Palestine
7BM	Complete Uncirculated Mill Set	1908-1917	Palestine
8BM	10 Pruth ICllircul. Coins	1949	
9BM	Collection of Ancient Coins (Replica); 1 Telephone Token		
10BM	2 Gold Plated Moshe Dayan Medals	1948	Jerusalem
11BM	Collection of 20 Coins (Silver & Gold)	1366-1935	Palestine
12BM	Music—Artzzenu Tango (Solo Piano) (Z. Zahavi, E. Goldberg)		Tel Aviv
13BM	Music—Anachnu (Solo—Original Script) (M. Bick Agency)		Palestine; New York
14BM	Music—Batzir (Solo) (D. Samborsky)		Montreal
15BM	Music—Laylah (Solo) (M. Zeira)		Montreal
16BM	"Illegal" Immigrants on Haganah Ship (2 pictures)	1947	

17BM	Hebrew Dictionary	1936	Mizpah Publ. Co., Palestine
18BM	Jewish Symbols on Ancient Jewish Coins	1971	A.I.N.A., New York
19BM	Bank Note (500 Prutah)		Palestine
20BM	Bank L'Evni Le-Israel (500 Prutah)	1935-45	Palestine
23BM	Hallah Cover—Great Palestine Orpah-Asyllum Diskin Society		Jerusalem

William Hauben

Theodor Herzl

No.	Object Name	Date	Source
1TH	The Delegates, First Zionist Congress (picture)	1897 & Gold Medal	Basle
2TH	First Zionist Congress in Action (picture)	1903	Jewish National Fund
3TH	Theodor Herzl (signed picture)	May 1903	
4TH	A Selection of 6 Herzl Medals		
5TH	Hatikvah—Victor Military Band (Victor Co. recording)	1903	
6TH	Hatikvah (Solo/Piano)	1908	J. Mber Publ., A. Teres, N.Y.
7TH	Zion Songs (Solo/Piano), (Hatikvah & dort Vu Die Zeder)	1918	S. Schenker, N.Y.
8TH	The Old New Home (Music)	1927	S. Chesney Publ.
9TH	Hadassah (Daughters of Zion)	1929	A. Podnos Publ.
10TH	T. Herzl—100 Lire Banknote	1968	State of Israel
11TH	T. Herzl (9 pages including historical pictures)		
12TH	Theodor Herzl in Memorial Book (pictures/diaries/articles)	1929	New Palestine— Manuf. In U.S.A.
13TH	Herzl—Book	1975	Elon, Amos; Holt, Rinehard, Publ.
14TH	Hatikvah (hand writing)	1918	J. Roskin (arranged)
15TH	Herzl Tomb (photo)		Jerusalem
15TH-I	M'zuza in olive wood holder	1936	Palestine

Ben-Gurion

No.	Description	Date/Source
1BG	David Ben-Gurion—First Prime Minister (with signatures)	State of Israel
2BG	Prof. Chayim Weizman—First President (with signatures)	State of Israel
3BG	Menachem Begin—Prime Minister (with signatures)	State of Israel
4BG	Yitzchak Navon—President (with signature)	State of Israel
5BG	Declaration of Independence (with signatures)	5/5/48
6BG	Ben-Gurion & Family (photo album)	Tel Aviv, 1957
7BG	Israel at 30 (photo album)	Jerusalem (1948-1978)
8BG	Cities of Israel, etc.—15 pictures (copy of original prints)	
9BG	Eastward-Hymn of the Land of Israel (sheet music)	P. Jassinkowsky, Renanah Music N.Y.
10BG	50 Shequalim (1 sheet of 12 banknotes)	Bank of Israel
11BG	Pre-Israeli Stamps (8 sheets)	Israel, 1946
12BG	Pre-Israeli Stamps (12 sheets)	Israel, 1946
13BG	Pastures in the Wilderness—Ben-Gurion	Jewish National Fund, 11/28/48
14BG	Jewish National Fund Stamps	Dept. of Education, N.Y.
15BG	Victory Stamps—Western Wall (4 sheets)	Israel, 1967
16BG	First Day Cover—Album	1939-1945, March 1976
17BG	The Jerusalem Post—War to Peace	1973-1993
18BG	32nd World Zionist Congress Edition	7/18/92

19BG	The Israel Flag	Jewish National Fund
20BG	Keren Kayemet Le Israel	Jewish National Fund
21BG	Rabin, Arafat, President Clinton (newspaper photo)	Jerusalem Post
22BG	Rabin, Arafat, President Clinton (newspaper photo)	Tampa Tribune
23BG	Honor Roll—Jewish National Fund (special edition, pictures)	Israel
24BG	Keren Hayesod (data, 1920-1948)	K. Hajesod, Jerusalem
25BG-X	25th Anniversary Silver Coin of Israeli Independence (Ben-Gurion)	
26BG-X	"The Vision and the Way"—#0218— Sterling Silver Medal (Ben-Gurion)	
27BG-X	Ben-Gurion Centennial Bronze Medal, 1886-1986	Israeli Coin & Medal Corp.
28BG-X	Independence Coin, Jerusalem Capital of Israel, Silver Coin, 1977	Israeli Coin & Medal Corp.
29BG-X	Keren Hayesod—25th Anniversary Bronze Medal, 1920-1970	Israeli Coin & Medal Corp.